The Queen's Envoy

Extracts from the Oh So Secret Diaries of Lord David

By Lord David Prosser
Author of *My Barsetshire Diary*

~~~~~~~~~~~~~

United Kingdom – United States – Australia
~~~~~~~~~~~~~

LIBRARY OF CONGRESS CATALOGING-IN-PUBLICATION DATA

Title: The Queen's Envoy: Extracts from the Oh So Secret Diaries of Lord David
ISBN: 978-1-4475-1181-6
Date of Publication: 2011
Printed in the United Kingdom

Table of Contents

Forward by Lord David Prosser.....7

Thursday, January 17, 1991
Who's the Daddy!.....9

Friday, January 18, 1991
The Solicitor's Promise.....11

Saturday, January 19, 1991
Lords Above!.....13

Sunday, January 20, 1991
Breaking the News.....17

Monday, January 21, 1991
The Visitor Arrives.....19

Wednesday, Jan 23, 1991
The Wad of Money.....21

Friday, January 25, 1991
The Oil Treaty.....23

Saturday, January 26, 1991
Russian Face Off.....27

Sunday, January 27, 1991
The Threat of the Latex Glove.....33

Monday January, 28, 1991
The Thought of Murder.....37

Wednesday, January 30, 1991
The Theft of Socks.....39

Monday, Nov 25, 1991
Bertie Returns.....43

Tuesday, November 26, 1991
The Frosty Reception.....45

Wednesday November 27, 1991
The Perils of Prunella.....47

Thursday, November 28, 1991
Alvin and the Chipmunks.....51

Friday, November 29, 1991
Lost On My Way to the Kitchen.....53

Saturday, November 30, 1991
Joyous Homecoming.....61

Sunday, December 1, 1991
The Lord and Religion.....65

Sunday, December 8, 1991
The Birthday.....71

Wednesday, December 25, 1991
Christmas Day.....75

Thursday January 2, 1992
Nightmare in Gay Paree, or How I became the Crow.....83

Friday, January 3, 1992

Fashion Parade.....91
Saturday, January 4, 1992
A Chance Encounter.....95

Sunday, January 5, 1992
The Quick Trim.....101

Wednesday, July 15, 1992
Departure and the Birthday Pillow.....107

Monday, October 4, 1993
Sir Bertie and the Indiscreet Letters.....115

Tuesday, October 5, 1993
The Subtle Taxi Driver.....121

Wednesday, October 6, 1993
If I Told You I'd Have to Kill You.....123

Thursday, October 7, 1993
The Heir Hunter.....127

Friday, October 8, 1993
Cold Packs for the Pain.....131

Saturday, October 9, 1993
The Superb Play.....133

Sunday, October 10, 1993
A Walk in the Park.....135

Monday, October 11, 1993
A Royal Blush.....139

Tuesday, October 12, 1993

Hitting the Jackpot at Home.....143
Monday, September 5, 1994
The Results.....149

Tuesday, September 6, 1994
The Pianist.....151

Thursday, July 8, 1999
A Room with a View.....155

Friday, July 9, 1999
Mustapha Asks a Favor.....163

Saturday, July 10, 1999
The Holiday-Day.....167

Sunday, July 11, 1999
Knife in the Night.....173

Monday, July 12, 1999
The Infection.....183

Foreword
By Lord David Prosser

I know that most biographies will enthral you with the childhood and early life of the subject. Some will entertain, some will enthral and others will thrill. Mine would only bore.

Suffice it to say that I was born, was schooled and then I worked. That way I shall not bore you Dear Readers, and we can get to the meat of this, my life.

We shall start this story at my rebirth, when all things changed and adventure began. So, Dear Reader, I offer you my world from when it was new and a Lord was born. So, let's view some of my diary entries from that time.

I would like to thank the following people to whom this book is dedicated.

Ilil Arbel, without whose prodding I might never have written. Blame Her!

Gary Morgenstein, for letting me bend his car and for accepting my friendship.

Kenn Gold, for taking a chance on an unknown writer and publishing a new work.

Lis Eastwood, for ensuring my English was the right side of the channel.

Pauline Yudowitz. The word *NICE* was written for her, someone who prompted me to try and encouraged me despite reading a chapter.

Michael Frankel, for being a good brother and letting me insult his cars.

James Parris For his real friendship and good humour

Lee James, Jen, and my Brother Dilwyn for being my family, poor fools.

My nieces Karen and Joanne for their constant nagging which kept me indoors a lot.

Lady Victoria, with thanks for suggesting I have a sense of fun. Enjoy it.

My wife Julia and Daughter Yvonne, for being who they are and supporting me when I was a starving writer by keeping the sandwiches and coffee coming.

Thursday, January 17, 1991
Who's the Daddy!

What an excellent birthday. I had taken a few days off work to make this a long weekend. By 10 am I had followed Ysabel round the house and the local streets carefully removing all signs that said '40 TODAY', as I considered that I could manage without the advertising. At age fourteen, I don't think she understood the full meaning of discretion.

We had an excellent lunch at The Flying Pig, and I even indulged in a pint of bitter. Needless to say, I wore my birthday gifts for the occasion.

From Ysabel, fluorescent orange socks with 'Who's the Daddy?' written on them, and a heavily flowered shirt in turquoise designed to make me 'cool'.

From Julia a pair of jeans indicative of her urge to bring me into the twentieth century. Also, a new waistcoat which was reminiscent of our old brocade curtains but which she knew I loved, which reminded me to check to see if we still had the curtains later.

We got home at about 4.00 pm just in time to catch the phone ringing. It was my solicitor's secretary asking if we would be available to call in at twelve o'clock the following day. I was off work with no set plans so I agreed.

Recently I had learned that my father's, mother's, brother's son, whom I couldn't decide was my second cousin or my first cousin once removed, was ill and close to the end. His name was Enoch (pronounced E-noch rather than Ee-noch as some say) and I'd never met him but it was likely that I would be asked to make his funeral arrangements.

The rest of today was quiet, interrupted only by people phoning with birthday wishes and the usual jokes about my life going downhill from here on in. An episode from X-Files and I was ready for bed, that is, once I could persuade the damned cat to unoccupy it first.

Friday, January 18, 1991
The Solicitor's Promise

Julia drove me into Barchester and we arrived at Mr Figg-Newton's at 12.00 prompt. He was waiting for us in the reception and ushered us into his room. I was fully expecting to hear about the death of my... relative, but was surprised when he said, “Well, Mr. Prosser, what are we to do? It seems your little bump in the car last week occurred with the wife of a councillor of Praisewater close to where you live. She's suggesting the damage was quite severe and is considering court action. What would you like me to do?”

I saw Julia's expression which looked explosive so I quickly responded to the question.

“Mr Figg-Newton”, said I. “I want you to accept that my wife was not responsible for the accident. We were both in the car when it happened, and not only was our car not moving, it was actually in a parking bay at the local supermarket. I should point out that this idiot woman actually caught our rear light but all she sustained was a small scratch along the side of her car”.

“I see”, said Mr Figg-Newton. “So her claim that her front light and bumper were damaged is untrue?”

“Indeed”, I said, “she cornered sharply in the car park, hit our rear light with the passenger side of her car and ran on a few feet leaving scratches. I have no doubt that she's had another accident since then and is hoping to find an idiot to pay for it all”.

“I shall look into this further”, said Mr Figg-Newton showing us to the door. “I shall be in touch anon”.

Julia was seething somewhere just south of the boiling point. It wouldn't take much for her to drive into

Praisewater and seek out the councillor and his devious wife. I distracted her with the thought of some new shoes and more so with a new bridle for the horse.

At 3.00 pm we were home again. Though we hadn't stopped on the journey, I noticed she glanced at the Praisewater Council offices as we passed through.

I settled on the couch for a while with a coffee, Oscar having appropriated my chair, or, what he actually considered to be one of his. I was glancing through the local paper while Julia adjusted the bridle and Ysabel, now home from school, taught Joey the budgie how to drink from her cola tin in order to watch him having hiccups.

At 4.00 pm the phone rang. Again it was Mr Figg-Newton's secretary asking me to call again on the following day at 12.00. I was surprised to find him working on a Saturday but I agreed to go.

After dinner we had a game of Trivia which I won, having a good memory for such fluff. I refused to play Monopoly on the grounds I never won and always ended up declaring myself bankrupt after about twenty minutes, while everyone else had multi storey hotels on their Water Works just waiting to catch me. And I swear my criminal record must have been second to none, considering the amount of times I had to “Go Directly to Jail without passing Go”.

Saturday, January 19, 1991
Lords Above!

I attended Mr Figg-Newton at 12.00, fully expecting him to require a written statement about the accident. He'd surprised me by asking to see me alone and so I passed my wallet to Julia, feeling its fear the while, and told her to go round a shop she liked and I'd catch her up - hopefully before my wallet expired from lack of funds.

Mr Figg-Newton ushered me into his office with a "Please enter and sit sir", which I found strangely formal. I did so.

"You are aware that your relative has been ill", he said. I nodded agreement. "It is my duty to inform you that he has passed away, My Lord".

"My Lord? Mr Figg-Newton, what do you mean?"

He told me that my cousin had been Lord of the Manor of Bouldnor, and, as the eldest male and because there was no named successor, the title now fell to me. Though it did not make me a Peer of the Realm, and did not come with an estate, I retained the rare privilege of being able to grant a market should I so wish. At that I think I felt a little underwhelmed. He did remind me that the bearing of a title carried certain duties to which I had given no thought, and I rapidly developed a feeling of responsibility. I received a document from him verifying the transfer of the title and made to leave.

He stopped me with a gesture. "By the way", he said, "I almost forgot. I phoned the other driver this morning. I accidentally referred to you as Lord Prosser before I'd told you, and she suddenly decided to take no further action. Said she'd pay for the repairs herself. Edna something or other, strange woman. A good news day all round for you".

I met Julia at the store and we headed for the coffee bar. I was pleased to see not too many bags and my wallet breathed a sigh of delight as it was returned safely. I sat her down and went to order two lattes. By the time the young lady on the counter had run the verbal gamut of all the choices available with and without syrups, I'd almost changed my mind. Eventually I ordered two plain lattes. I returned to the table and sat down.

"Right My Lady", I said to Julia, "your latte is on its way".

She looked at me a little oddly.

"Lady Julia Prosser of Bouldnor, may I introduce myself? Lord David Prosser of Bouldnor, delighted to make your acquaintance".

By now I could see she was considering that her next purchase should be a strait jacket pour moi, so I gave her the news. Ever the pragmatist, all she replied was, "Well, we've not lived in the village very long. The locals will adjust".

We had in fact only moved in a month ago to be closer to my job in Local Government as the daily travelling was getting to be too much. It occurred to me then to wonder how my employer and colleagues would react when I passed on my news. I guessed they'd react quite well if I kept the cheering down as I handed in my notice.

Julia and I, (Ysabel having gone to a friend for the night) decided to celebrate with a visit to the local pub. Lady J, as I now called her, had a red wine and I had a half pint of the local brew which is guaranteed to have you on your knees doing Toulouse Lautrec impressions after two glasses.

Smiley Jackson, the landlord of the Fursty Ferret, brought the drinks to the table.

“On the house, My Lord”, he said. (Twenty years later and I still don't know how he knew).

After two glasses of wine and three halves of local brew, Lady J took me home. Somehow I seem to have learned a new song about a mademoiselle from Armentieres?

Sunday, January 20, 1991
Breaking the News

Lady J was busy phoning round to let the family know what had happened. My nieces were delighted, especially when she explained I was still Uncle David to them. Her sister Mumu is married to Baron Caslav, and while he was delighted at the news, she seemed less so. That was not unusual as they are very competitive girls. There is no doubt that they love each other dearly and if either were in trouble the other would be there, but the rest of the time, sight or sound of each other could make a person's hair stand on end. There are barbs in every sentence they speak to each other, just waiting to entangle any fool stupid enough to try and intervene. I remember Mumu saying "Oh how nice dahling, now you can join the upper echelons of society". Julia later translated this for me to mean "at least you won't be peasants anymore".

We ate at home that day as I had a slight headache, which I put down to the shock of the previous day or so. I spent much of the day lying down and contemplating my future. Julia spent much of the day on the various phone calls and Ysabel taught Joey how to play football with an old ping-pong ball.

Monday, January 21, 1991
The Visitor Arrive

I took Lady J her bucket of coffee quite early this morning in case she decided to go to the stables. Oscar decided to say he loved me by entwining himself around my ankles on my way out of the bedroom. Down I went.

My head now on a level with his, I received a head butt and a miaow loud enough to remind me I hadn't fed him. That's what I love about Oscar, his subtlety.

I had a shower after feeding the cat and although I knew it wasn't yet eight, I heard Lady J take a phone call. As I came out to get dressed she told me she'd received an odd call from a man asking that I made sure I was available and at home at 9.00 am.

As Julia went off to see to her horse, I settled with a coffee to wait. At 9.00 promptly there was a knock at the door. I answered it to find on my doorstep a gentleman dressed in a smart pinstripe suit.

"Good morning, My Lord", he said, "I am Bertram Threadneedle, and I should be most grateful for a few minutes of your time".

I invited him in and waved him through to the lounge. I just knew that wherever he sat it would leave his suit covered in grey hair from Oscar as all seats were of course his. He declined a coffee so I sat down to finish mine while he talked.

"How can I help you, Mr. Threadneedle?" I asked.

"Actually it's Sir Bertram", he said, "and I'm here on behalf of Her Majesty's Government. I don't know if you're aware that your cousin, Lord Roberts of Bouldnor, did, on occasion, do some small errands on behalf of Her

Majesty in a diplomatic fashion where the government could not act directly. He was sort of a roving diplomat”.

“I was not aware of this, but pray continue”, I said.

“There was a delicate task your late cousin had agreed to help with that we hope you might undertake for us as his successor”.

“Of course”, I replied, “if there's a way in which I might help, please don't hesitate to tell me”.

“Marvellous”, he responded. “Then if your passport is up to date I shall have a case file and some travel documents sent over”.

Passport? Travel documents? What did he mean? Leaving me a little dazed, Sir Bertram got up, shook my hand and left. I was on the doorstep watching him get into a chauffeured Rolls Royce before I came out of the daze, too late to ask questions.

When Julia returned later I tried to explain what had happened, but as laconic as ever, all I got from her was, “You have your duty David, I'm sure you'll do it well”.

Wednesday, Jan 23, 1991
The Wad of Money

Later in the morning the Rolls Royce returned with a file of photographs and documents plus an itinerary and tickets for travel. They even included a wad of money in English pounds and Beritana dinars. The photographs confirmed that Beritana was my destination and showed me pictures of a palace and of various people there. I viewed them all and then tested myself on them. Quite good really, I remembered one name in three and even attached it to the right person sometimes.

The documents told me that there had been a new oil find there and the UK was anxious to own it. It would have been my late cousin's job to persuade the sultan to let us buy it. It seemed my late cousin was quite important and I was a little flummoxed that they'd asked me to take his place. I read that Sultan Ibrahim had a British wife and a young daughter and that he had been educated in England. That was handy as I didn't speak Arabic.

Lady J came back from the stables and we decided to eat out at Cass E Dees, a local cafe. I know we ate, but the problem on my mind of how to succeed in this mission made me forget what. I do remember at some stage Lady J saying, "Don't be so silly David, of course you can do it", before the subject was officially dropped.

At home again a little later, Sir Bertram arrived and I was fully expecting him to apologise and say that there had been a mistake and that a more suitable candidate had been found. Instead he was short, sharp and to the point.

"You leave on Friday, My Lord. Good luck in your endeavours which I leave entirely in your hands", he said, leaving me stunned and speechless.

After he had left I set Julia and Ysabel the task of sorting me out a suitcase and packing the right clothes. I asked them to let me know if I needed anything. I just sat there in shock.

Friday, January 25, 1991
The Oil Treaty

Lady J dropped me at the airport at 7.45 am. All would have been OK if I hadn't noticed that I'd forgotten my passport. I phoned home and asked Ysabel to call a taxi and have it delivered to me as quickly as possible. I didn't want her to lie to Julia but I did hope that she'd forget to mention it to her, or that Julia herself suffered amnesia before I got back.

Anyway, the taxi arrived complete with passport with half an hour to spare. Then, because I'd explained the problem to the cabin crew, they'd agreed to bend the rules for me, Lord David. But, I hadn't had time to change my passport and was expecting to be summarily ejected. Luckily for me Ysabel had placed the solicitor's letter inside so that I could verify that I was who I'd said.

I settled into my seat and awaited take-off. I was still very nervous about the whole journey and the thought of letting my country down. The stewardess didn't make me feel any better when she started waving her arms like a windmill and talking about emergency chutes, and worse still, sick-bags. I asked for a drink.

The journey to Saudi took forever. This was mainly due to the fact that I was sitting next to a sweet old lady (from hell) who insisted I share her joy by showing me photographs of her grandchildren. Every pocket in her coat and her hand luggage was full of pictures. I was able to follow each child from meal to meal, from going to bed to getting up, from school gate going in to school gate coming out again. The pictures alone must have covered her entire baggage allowance. I knew the children's ages, shoe sizes and favourite meals.

After what seemed like two years the plane finally landed and I was able to say goodbye to grandma. I disembarked, entered the airport terminal and found my suitcase on the carousel. I walked over to the customs desk.

"You bring alcohol?" asked the officer.

"No", I replied.

"You have dirty pictures?" he asked.

"No", I replied.

"You go", he said looking sad. I felt almost guilty at disappointing him.

Out on the concourse I looked for the person who'd been despatched to meet me. I saw people carrying signs for 'Herren Baumfart und Schwartz', 'Ivana Gohome', 'Lord Daud', 'Smith and Jones'... just a minute, Lord Daud? Could that be me?

I approached the chap holding the sign and expecting the same lack of English I'd experienced with customs officers and their learned lines, said, "Me Daud. Go Beritana yes?"

"Ah wonderful", came the response. "Allow me to introduce myself old chap. Mustapha Phag at your service. I'm the sultan's factotum and will drive you to Beritana and the palace".

Dumbfounded and not a little embarrassed I offered my hand.

"Delighted to meet you", I stuttered.

He escorted me to a vintage Rolls Royce and our journey started.

"There will be only one other guest", he told me. "He's a Russian envoy called Mikhail Gottakov. Pleasant chappie".

Mustapha pointed out various sites on our three hour drive to the border; they were few and far between as it was mostly deserted. To be honest, most of the sites he pointed out seemed to me to be desert as well.

At the border the car was waved through, and after that it was less than an hour to Beritana's capital, Beritana City, and to the palace.

The palace itself was a magnificent edifice standing on a small hill at the centre of the city, with all other buildings radiating out from it. Built of what looked like pink blocks of stone, it was lit up by floodlights from below and seemed to shine. If it was intended to impress it did its job.

Servants dashed to the car as we drew up. They seemed to squabble over my single suitcase. I was shown to my rooms by Mustapha who informed me he'd see me later at dinner which would be at eight and would be very informal. As it was by then almost six o'clock I decided to relax on the bed for a while. I must have dozed off because the next thing I knew there was a man shaking me and asking if I wished to shower before dinner. I did so and was escorted downstairs to eat wearing an informal cream linen suit which appeared to have been freshly ironed.

Sultan Ibrahim himself greeted me in what I assumed was the dining room.

"Come in, old chap, and make yourself comfortable", he said, indicating a variety of cushions at floor level by very low tables.

"Thank you, Your Highness", I replied.

"No, no dear Bouldnor", he said, "call me Ibrahim, and allow me to present my wife Jenny". He indicated towards a slim, pretty, blonde woman of about his age, which I remembered reading was thirty.

"Enchanted, Your Highn..er Jenny", I said.

"I'm pleased to meet you too, Lord David", she said. "So nice to meet someone from home".

Although amongst all the Etonian accents I'd been hearing, I was surprised she ever got the chance to miss England at all.

Over dinner, which was lamb with rice, I was also introduced to Gottakov, saw Mustapha again and met a few of the sultan's dignitaries. Gottakov was a short man who had adopted the wearing of a pince-nez, and while pleasant to speak to, did appear to be a rather picky and pedantic man.

After the meal everyone chatted generally. It really was a very informal affair. Ibrahim asked Gottakov and me if we had considered wearing the typical Bedouin robes for comfort in the heat, to which I replied that had I been able to avail myself of some in the UK, then I should have been delighted to adopt this method of attire during my trip. Gottakov said he preferred his suits.

Soon afterwards we all retired for the night, Ibrahim saying he would see us tomorrow.

Saturday, January 26, 1991
Russian Face Off

I woke quite early this morning. After stepping into the shower I heard someone enter my room. I washed quickly and stepped out to find Mustapha sitting on my bed.

"Morning old man", he said. "Ibrahim sends you his greetings and a gift. Some Bedouin robes for you to try".

"I'm overwhelmed at His Highness's kindness", I replied. "I'll be happy to try them if you can give me a moment to dress".

"His Highness hopes you will join him on the battlements before breaking your fast, David", he said. I dressed quickly, finding the robes most comfortable, and then Mustapha led the way to the battlements.

"Ibrahim is hawking", he told me.

"Oh dear, I do hope he's not ill", I replied, misunderstanding.

Mustapha seemed to find this hilarious. "No, no old chap, I mean he's flying his hawk". And indeed he was. It was a magnificent bird. I saw it swooping in the air as I approached and then return to its master's gloved hand.

"Good morning Daud", said Ibrahim, adopting the Arabic equivalent of my name. "A most beautiful day don't you think?"

I agreed and told Ibrahim how much I admired his skill with the hawk.

"It's a marsh harrier", he told me, "and coming along nicely in training". He called to an elderly man to come and take the bird. The man came and transferred the bird to his own hand, and gripping the jess tightly, put a hood on the bird and then took it back to the mews where it was kept.

“Come”, said Ibrahim, “lets breakfast together”. Mustapha and I followed him in.

This morning the table was laden with fruit. With just the three of us there, Ibrahim asked me what I thought of his country. I told him that what I had seen of it looked wonderful. He told me that he wanted to do great things with his people and intended to start with education. I said I thought that was the way forward for all people.

At that moment Gottakov came in and wished us all good morning. He sat and joined us as we wished him the best of the day.

No sooner had he started to eat than a young child, probably about four years of age, came in. Without a word she rushed over to Gottakov and plumped herself in his lap. She plumped, he jumped.

“Go away child”, he said. “Have you no manners?” I saw a smile play about Ibrahim's lips as the child got up from where Gottakov had unceremoniously dumped her when he jumped. (I hope you appreciate my poetry here, plumped, jumped and dumped).

She looked at him with disdain and then turning in my direction launched herself into my lap. With a bit of a wriggle she made herself comfy and picked up a few grapes from the table. She dropped one in her mouth and then selecting another from the bunch dropped one in mine too.

“Why thank you little one”, I said. “And what's your name?”

“I'm Suki”, she replied, and then repeated her formula with the grapes, one each.

I stroked Suki's head unconsciously. She was a pretty little girl and obviously very lively. She was obviously well liked as neither Ibrahim nor Mustapha had berated her for coming in.

“I'm four”, said Suki. “How old are you?”

“Suki”, said Ibrahim, “that's a rude question to ask”.

“I don't mind, Your Highness”, I told him, and then to Suki, “I'm for.....ty”.

“That's old”, she said and I couldn't help but burst out laughing.

“Lord Daud”, said Ibrahim, “I’m afraid my daughter can be a little forward at times. Please forgive her rudeness”.

“Your Highness”, I told him, “my own daughter was such a delight as this at the same age. There's nothing to forgive”.

As breakfast ended Suki took my hand and asked if I'd like to meet her pony. I answered that I'd be delighted if her Daddy didn't need me. The Sultan who obviously indulged his wonderful daughter gave his permission and told her not to keep me too long as he needed to talk with me later.

With giggles she led me away and I spent a delightful hour being shown round the Royal Stables and meeting her horse Nightshade. She was an adorable child. After the tour she took me by the hand again and led me indoors. All the servants smiled as they saw her. Jenny appeared and with a pretend scowl said she'd been looking for Suki for ages. “Such a terrible, wilful child”, she said with a smile.

I made my way back to the dining hall where I found Mustapha.

“Would you like to go to the throne room?” he asked. “You can see His Highness dispense his justice and his wisdom”.

We watched Ibrahim all morning and he treated all who came before him with seriousness and fairness. He dispensed justice like a modern Solomon and no one complained at all.

In the afternoon Mustapha showed me the city and some Roman aqueducts that carried the water for the city from some distant hills. We returned to the palace at about six o'clock where I was greeted by Suki rushing up and asking me to come to dinner. Following her lead I came to the dining room where I found her father and mother waiting.

"Ha", said Ibrahim, "she brings a friend hoping for support when she refuses to eat her vegetables". Jenny and he burst into laughter.

I sat with Suki and watched as she manipulated food onto a fork. She managed to get it to her mouth and eat it. The next forkful also contained what looked like some carrots and she offered it to me.

"No thank you sweetie, I can already see in the dark", I told her.

Puzzled, she asked why, and I said it was because I ate my vegetables.

She ate the forkful herself.

"Can we put the lights out, Daddy, to see if it works?" she asked.

We were all laughing as I explained that it took more than one mouthful to accomplish it.

She ate the rest of her meal without complaint though I was offered the occasional forkful out of kindness, I think.

After the meal we all wished her goodnight and left her with her servant who would take her to bed. We then settled down to our own meal, at which point I noticed that Gottakov was missing. I enquired of Mustapha where Gottakov was and he told me that now a decision regarding the oil was made, Gottakov had left for Russia. I was very surprised as nothing had been said. I was also disappointed as it was obvious my mission had failed.

The meal went well and I made every effort to chat despite my feelings. Afterwards I said I would return home on the following day and wished everyone a goodnight. I went to my room to complete my diary before going to sleep.

Sunday, January 27, 1991
The Threat of the Latex Glove

The airport in Saudi was very helpful in finding me a flight when I phoned. I rang Julia and asked her to meet my plane and went down to breakfast.

This morning Ibrahim was missing. Mustapha told me he had been called away urgently and I knew that it was really so that he didn't have to speak to me. After breakfast Jenny and Suki came to say goodbye to me and Mustapha brought the Rolls Royce round to take me to the airport.

During the ride back to Saudi, Mustapha chatted and asked if I'd enjoyed my trip. I thanked him and said I'd enjoyed it very much, although I regretted not having been able to talk to Ibrahim. He ignored this opportunity to explain why the decision over the oil had been made without me having had the chance to put my case.

When we reached the airport Mustapha offered me his hand. I shook it gladly as I had found him a pleasant companion. Inside the airport I bought myself some cigarettes to hide from Julia, some perfume for Julia and some nail varnish for Ysabel.

The plane was on time and the journey was nice and easy. Not a doting grandmother in sight. At home I collected my case and headed for the 'Nothing to Declare' line. A grim looking officer beckoned me over and asked if I had anything to declare. I answered in the negative and forbore asking him why he thought I'd chosen that line.

"No cigarettes?" he asked.

"Two hundred only", I replied.

"No alcohol?"

"None", I said.

"Gifts?" he asked.

“Just some perfume and nail varnish”, I replied. I thought that would be it but he asked me to open my case. Of course this was just the action to make me start feeling worried and I knew I had started to sweat. I was nervous as I opened the case for him even though I knew I'd done nothing wrong. The more he looked through the case the more nervous I became in case someone had planted something there. He noticed my nervousness and said he was just going to speak to someone.

He returned moments later with another officer who was cheerfully donning a pair of latex gloves. I was beginning to fear the worst when I heard him say “Thank you, My Lord, you're clear to go”.

I'm sure I must have sighed with relief which no doubt made him more suspicious, but it was too late; I grabbed my suitcase and was gone.

Julia met me at the gate and we hugged. “I just asked where you were”, she told me, “and some funny little chap carrying a box of latex gloves said he'd find out”. I hugged my saviour again.

On the journey home we chatted about my trip. I said I had been unsuccessful but couldn't understand what I'd done wrong, and why Ibrahim hadn't found time to speak to me. I told her all about the people I'd met and all about little Suki.

“I'm sure you did your very best my dear”, she told me comfortingly.

"My best was obviously not good enough", I replied."Sir Bertram will no doubt be disappointed and will never ask me to represent the government again".

We arrived home at about five and in a spontaneous burst, picked up Ysabel and went for a pizza. Lady J told me that while I'd been gone she'd engaged a housekeeper called Grizelda who would start on the following day.

When we got in I said I wanted an early night, gave the girls their gifts and went to unpack my case and hide the cigarettes.

Monday January, 28, 1991
The Thought of Murder

It was about 8.00 am when I felt a presence by my bed. I realised dimly that I had not taken Lady J her coffee, and in a semi panic swung my legs out of bed with my eyes still closed. I heard a sharp intake of breath and opened my eyes. There stood a strange woman trying desperately to avert her eyes as I made an equally desperate attempt to reach my dressing gown with my toes and slip it on. I managed it.

Before I could ask the woman who she was and what she wanted in my bedroom, she spoke.

"Telephone, My Lord. It's a Sir Bertram and he said it's urgent".

I went to the phone, realisation slowly dawning that this must be Grizelda.

"David, old chap, I'll be with you at nine o'clock, OK?" Without waiting for a reply he hung up leaving me spluttering.

Grizelda informed me that Lady Julia had gone to 'er 'orse and asked if I'd like a coffee. I thanked her and said that that would be very nice and asked her to leave it in the lounge for me. I'd get it when I came back from dressing.

I showered and dressed quickly and by 8:55 I was enjoying my coffee in the lounge. A knock at the door came and I saw Grizelda go to answer it. Within moments she was back with Sir Bertram in tow.

I was ready to apologise for my lack of success in Beritana when he stopped me in my tracks.

"Congratulations, my dear chap", he said, "Her Majesty's Government is in your debt. We couldn't believe you managed it so quickly. Sultan Ibrahim asked me to pass on his thanks for the attention you paid his daughter who was, it seems, captivated with you. Beritana will welcome you at any time".

"Ah, hm, it was nothing", I said, a little bemused. I'd managed it. How? However, grateful that I'd somehow managed to succeed in the mission, I didn't voice that thought.

Sir Bertram repeated his thanks and asked if I'd be willing to undertake further missions. He seemed delighted when I agreed. I was delighted that he'd asked. He shook hands and left, promising to be in touch.

When Julia returned I was still all smiles and able to tell her of my success.

"I already know my dear", she said, "I had a call when you left Beritana from someone called Mustapha Phag. He said he'd forgotten to tell you of the decision, but I thought I'd better wait until you heard officially".

I thought for a moment that this would be a justifiable reason for murder.

Wednesday, January 30, 1991
The Theft of Socks

The day dawned bleak and cold. For me, it also dawned far too early. I couldn't tell the exact time as I was unable to open my eyes. This was due to the fact that the cat had his nose, very cold and very wet, against one of them. There were two paws with needle sharp claws holding on to my cheeks and a further two either side of my Adam's apple. Movement was not an option and yet I'm sure that's what he had in mind, as the nose seemed to be prodding my eye and the miaow I could hear was reaching fever pitch. I was between a rock and a hard place - he wanted me to move, I wanted to move, but movement would leave me open to several piercings and facial disfigurement. Gradually I started to move my head sideways in the hope he'd just step off onto a pillow. With a quick backhanded swipe at my nose, he did. I managed to force open my eyes to see a very indignant cat standing there. I took the hint and got up.

After I'd washed his dishes I laid out new food and took it through to the utility room where his (unused) bed is, and where we feed him. Just behind the door I noticed a dark mass. On checking it I found it to be made up of pairs of my socks now covered in a layer of grey cat hair. He'd obviously been stealing them from the washing basket and making a bed. I noticed two things:

1. They were all laundered socks.
2. Only my socks were there.

I didn't yet understand the significance of this.

At seven o'clock I took a bucket of coffee through to Lady J and called Ysabel for school. If Julia was going to the stables today she would drop Ysabel off on the way.

It was just coming up to eight o'clock when the fun began. Oscar started crying in the special tone he uses that tells us he's about to throw up (usually on the Chinese rug or someone's bed). At the same time I saw the postman approach with a parcel and I went to open the door for him. I had just reached the door and opened it with my hand held out ready for the parcel when Julia reached the door (which she thought I'd opened for her) holding an armful of cat which she propelled outside. I'm not sure who was most surprised. The postman who got an armful of howling cat in exchange for the parcel, Julia when she saw she'd just thrown a cat at someone or Oscar himself to find a stranger holding him.

Time stood still for a moment and then Oscar dropped to the floor and promptly kept his promise by throwing up directly where the postman's shoe would have been had he not backed off in shock just in time.

With a distinctly sour 'Hrrumph' the postman turned and walked away. I'd like to have been a fly on the wall when he returned to the depot later. I can imagine him saying, “And these maniacs threw a cat at me”.

Julia went to get something to clean the mess off the step. Oscar walked back in as though nothing had happened and settled in my chair. I walked in and opened my parcel.

At 8.30 am Lady J and Ysabel kissed me goodbye and left. Grizelda arrived and made me a coffee so I decided to check my mail on the computer. My mail box was chock a block so I started answering in date of receipt.

There were quite a few messages from friends and a few invitations to answer. I also had adverts and offers galore.

How on earth had I managed all this time without the benefits of a man-girdle to give me back the shape of my youth? If it came to that, how did they know that I wasn’t a youth, and therefore still have my shape?

There was a competition to win a car for which only my entrance fee of £20.00 was needed.

There was the opportunity to become a millionaire by helping Jacob O'Malley of Nigeria transfer his fortune from a locked account in the Seychelles. All I had to do was provide my account details for his bank and act as a guarantor that he was real. I could phone his bank on a mobile number to check his story. Yes, folks, I had just got off the banana boat the day before, I was bound to fall for that one.

One that surprised me was an invitation to join a pyramid selling scheme. Who God’s earth was going to buy a pyramid? Did these people think me stupid? Answers on a postcard please.

One offer I ignored was for the berry of a wonder bush that would replace food for those on a diet. The bush grew in the back of the darkest cave, on the highest mountain that's lit by moonlight only on the first Thursday of every month. I mean, it was bound to be endangered if it were that rare wasn’t it? I decided to pass!

Answering or ignoring my mail took me till noon. Grizelda asked if I'd like lunch but I decided to wait until Lady J returned. Within fifteen minutes she had. I asked if she'd like to go out for lunch and she jumped at the chance. I wasn't sure if that was an indication that she felt neglected or if it was a reflection on Grizelda's cooking.

We drove up to town and had a snack at The Plumbers, a little café that used to be a builders’ merchants. They do such specials as 'Chicken Bolt-i' and 'U-bend sausage rolls' but we settled for ham and tomato sandwiches with a coffee each.

Julia told me that she was pleased my trip had been a success and that she hoped I'd do it again. She added that it was only because it had seemed to interest me and not that she wanted to get rid of me.

From there we drove home in time for Ysabel's return from school. As she had no homework we settled to a game of scrabble which Ysabel won with the word RAZZ using a blank and getting on a triple word score. I'm still not sure about that word but she was adamant that it was real. After dinner we watched the re-run of an old comedy series until bedtime.

I then went to bed myself where I made sure that the door was shut, so that the decision of when to get up in the morning would be mine.

Monday, November 25, 1991
Bertie Returns

At 9.10 am I got a telephone call to ask me to be at home and available for ten o'clock. There would be only one person who would ask for such a thing at short notice and sure enough at ten o'clock Sir Bertram Threadneedle knocked at the door.

Grizelda showed him through to the lounge and then furnished us both with a coffee.

"No Lady J?" he asked.

"Due back soon but currently with the horse", I replied. "She only shows her face here long enough so that we don't let her room out".

"Good", he said surprisingly. "I have a mission for you, David, that is a little delicate and possibly a little dangerous".

"Oh", I said, "and why delicate?"

"Because it involves a woman, David, and I don't know how Lady J will feel".

"I'm sure she'll understand whatever it is, Bertie. Above all she trusts me".

He explained that he required me to fly to a place called Sanliurfa in Anatolia. There I would find a man who had set himself up as an old style Turkish pasha complete with a harem. The daughter of an important colonel in the British Army had gone missing in the area and it was possible that this chap had abducted her. I was needed to visit the area and see what I could find out.

Obviously I agreed to go, and as time was of the essence for this poor girl I agreed to leave the next day for Istanbul.

Sir Bertram had somehow anticipated this and handed me tickets and cash for the journey and for any bribes I needed to make. After giving me a folder containing details of the mission, he offered me his hand and left.

At noon Lady J arrived home. I asked Grizelda to prepare us some soup and took Julia through to the dining room ready. The soup arrived and Grizelda left us to eat in peace. I started to tell Julia all about the visit. She appeared to be far from surprised and merely said she wondered why it had taken them so long to use me again. All was going well until I mentioned the reason for the mission. "A woman", she said with arched eyebrows. "How close will you have to get to her?"

"I have no idea", I replied, "as close as circumstances warrant I suppose".

"I want no hanky-panky, David", she told me, which was a bit of a shock as I'd never looked at another woman since my marriage.

"Yes, my dear", seemed to be the only answer I could muster.

During the evening I packed a case and explained to Ysabel that I would be going away but would be back in time for her birthday on December 8th.

Tuesday, November 26, 1991
The Frosty Reception

Julia ran me to the airport in the morning. I wasn't quite sure what I'd done wrong but the atmosphere on the journey left icicles in my beard. When we arrived I tried to introduce a thaw by saying how much I'd miss her while away and already couldn't wait to get back. That elicited a 'Hmmph', a quick hug and then she was gone. I'd thought she was happy for me to take on these little jobs.

Inside the airport I showed my passport and ticket and was sent through to the departure lounge where I was able to get some duty-free cigarettes. I had a cup of tea while I waited for the flight to be called. There were lots of children in the lounge and as my flight was called, I saw a group of three playing a game of leap-frog. Passing them, I leaped over the one playing frog. Unfortunately I must have been heavier than I thought, as he went crashing to the ground. I spent minutes apologising to him and then to the irate parents before I was able to board the plane. My feeling of guilt intensified when the stewardess told me my ticket had been upgraded.

The flight to Istanbul was quite long, just over eight hours. When I arrived I was held up in customs while they compared the face in my passport to my actual face. There were lots of grunts and glances back and forth before they were finally assured that I was me. Then they started on my suitcase. It must have taken them ten minutes to rifle through it, though it wasn't large.

I found a taxi outside the terminal and asked the driver to take me to a nice hotel.

There I was at the 'Moulin Rouge' which was a name I hadn't been expecting to find here. The Toulouse

Lautrec posters looked strange outside but scarier still was the manager who looked exactly like the painter.

I had a drink and a meal in the restaurant and suffered a 'cancan' cabaret while I ate. Then I went up to my room from where I phoned the local museum and was lucky to find an English speaker. I explained that I was going to Sanliurfa to view the excavations nearby and asked if there were someone they could recommend who could help an English Lord there. After a little muttering in the background, the man told me there was a local lord in Sanliurfa who would know best. Would I like his telephone number?

Thanking them profusely I took the name and number which matched the ones I already had and I phoned. Luck still on my side, I got through to him personally. I explained that the museum in Istanbul had said that he may be able to help me find a suitable hotel and perhaps a good guide who knew the excavations. Not only did I get an invitation to visit but also to stay with him for a week, starting the next day.

I opened my case to get changed for bed and found that all my toiletries and my books had gone and my cigarettes had vanished. For a moment I wondered if Julia had arranged it.

Now I was going to get some sleep.

Wednesday November 27, 1991
The Perils of Prunella

The plane ride to Sanliurfa was rough, and so was the company. There were only eight seats on the plane which looked as though Von Richtofen might have been the last pilot. Each seat, bar mine, was occupied by rough unshaven men and even more unshaven women with an assortment of livestock on their knees. There were chickens and pigs and on my knee a goat. The pilot arrived. He looked bleary eyed and didn't appear to have shaved for a week, but he got the plane up and we arrived safely.

Outside the small airport building were three taxis. Seeing me emerge from the building all three drivers rushed over and tried simultaneously to grab my case. They were all jabbering in a dialect I didn't understand (I don't speak anything other than English and some schoolboy French). One of them eventually tried, "You H'Engerlish Mister?" which got enough of a response from me for him to grab the case and shoo away the others.

"Manchester United", he said, knowing that even I must understand that.

"Yes", I said.

"Where you go?" he asked.

"To Pasha Mehmet", I replied and I saw his face harden for a moment before he ushered me into his car.

"You friend Mehmet?" he asked.

"No", I answered, "but I'm a guest who wants to see the archaeological diggings here".

"Ah", he said as if that answered everything.

"My name Selim, you need car you call. I show you around". At which point he passed me a grubby card with his name and phone number and then started the engine.

Our journey to Mehmet's took almost an hour during which time Selim was smiling again and pointing out places of interest to me. Eventually we could see what looked like an old crusader fort atop a large hill. Selim pointed it out as our destination. His method of pointing didn't fill me full of confidence as he raised both hands from the wheel, said “Mehmet there”, and spat out of the window. He refused to drive through the gate as we drew up so I paid him there using American dollars and ensuring a big tip.

“You call if you need, ANYTIME”, he emphasised, and drove off.

As he did so, the largest man I'd ever seen approached me. He must have been fully 6'6” tall and almost as wide. There were cascades of fat over the top of his pants and his little waistcoat barely reached his sides. He was also completely bald. He bowed to me, picked up my case as though it weighed an ounce and gestured me to follow without a word.

We went through the gateway and across a large square where I could see guards in each corner carrying machine guns. In the centre was a fountain with a light display that looked out of place in such bleak surroundings.

We entered a large building on the far side of the square and my guide pointed towards a room using one hand to indicate that I should enter. He went off with my case.

I entered the room which was richly furnished with antiques from all parts of the world and with stands bearing what were obviously antiquities.

“Greetings, Lord Bouldnor”, I heard, and glancing towards a chair at the fireplace saw an arm inviting me forward.

There in the chair I found Mehmet. He was probably no more than five feet tall and though he had a full head of hair, he was almost as rotund as his servant.

"Greetings, Lord Mehmet" I said, "you are most kind to extend this invitation. Please call me David".

"Welcome", he replied, "here I am known as Pasha Mehmet".

I offered my hand which he shook limply.

"Sit, sit", he said. "Can I offer you a drink perhaps? Tea, coffee ,sherbet?"

"A tea would be most welcome", I replied.

Mehmet clapped his hands and the giant entered the room.

"Tea for two, Abdullah", Mehmet told him. To me he said, "My slave Abdullah cannot speak to you. He has no tongue. The reason for his bulk is because he is a eunuch".

I was surprised at the statement but made no comment. The way he had told me also left me glad I hadn't let my humour out for a trot by singing "And two for tea", when he spoke to Abdullah.

When the tea arrived we drank it as Mehmet talked about all his possessions and from whence they had come. It was strange, as he seemed to know exactly where they had come from and their dollar worth but he spoke without warmth. They were just possessions to brag about, not warm, beautiful objects to him. He did not impress me.

As the day grew on we went through to a smaller salon to eat. There was the usual low table and cushions on which to sit. The meal itself was wonderful and the courses were served by a succession of different men all quiet and taciturn. I had so far seen no women at all but decided not to pass comment.

Shortly afterwards, Mehmet wished me goodnight and had Abdullah show me to my allocated room. I thanked

Abdullah and he bowed and left. My bag was on the divan and I could see at once it had been searched. I wondered if Mehmet was suspicious of all his guests.

I decided to write my diary and bring you up to date, and then rested on the divan. The next day, I hoped to see more of the fort and to discover if Mehmet was holding Prunella Battersby, as the colonel's daughter was called.

Thursday, November 28, 1991
Alvin and the Chipmunks

I got up early this morning. From my window I could see the square and all the guards. There was no one in the passage outside my room so I decided to explore a bit. I showered and dressed first and then stepped out and shut my door. As I did so I noticed a red light flickering opposite and realised that there was a camera trained on my room. Pretending I hadn't seen it I walked along the passage way in the opposite direction to the way I'd approached it last night. I soon came to two sets of stairs. One led down, presumably to the rooms I'd been in yesterday, the study and dining rooms, or maybe the kitchen was there. The other stairs went up. Faintly from up there I could hear singing of a sort. I confess the voices I could hear were more reminiscent of Alvin and the Chipmunks played at 78rpm but they were still recognisable as those of women. I was tempted to go up but as I heard movement from below I chose to go down instead.

Mehmet must have been at the bottom, shouting at Abdullah. “Find him, you fool!” I heard. “Umh, umh, umh”, was the only reply.

As I appeared Mehmet stopped short, which was I suppose appropriate for someone his size.

“Good morning, Lord David”, he said, “It appears Abdullah has lost my favourite dog”, he improvised, but I knew he'd been referring to me.

Turning to Abdullah he just said “Go”.

“Would you like some help to look for the little fellow?” I ventured.

“Not necessary”, he told me, “I have plenty of slaves and servants to do that. Shall we take breakfast?”

I agreed and we entered the dining room together. I fully expected to see fruits on the table and was pleasantly surprised to see dishes containing bacon, fried eggs, tomatoes and mushrooms. With those and some toast I breakfasted well.

After breakfast Mehmet offered to take me to the local digs to view all the recent finds. I must admit that I was intrigued to see them and so I agreed. He led me outside to where a jeep had drawn up. Beside it was another large man who helped Mehmet into the front passenger seat. That was the long and short of it.

Oh dear, I thought, I must stop thinking about his shortcomings. Arrgh.

We spent most of the day at the excavations, some of which were situated in networks of caves in nearby hills. The finds were fascinating, and Mehmet told me that there were stories that this was the birth place of the biblical Abraham. People seemed friendly towards me but less so to Mehmet. Whenever his back was turned their expressions reflected that they held a very ‘low’ opinion of him. Oh dear, there I go again.

As we returned to the jeep for the journey back to the fort I noticed a number of boxes in the back. I said nothing, but a while after we returned I notice that more antiquities were displayed on low pillars in the study.

Dinner was again a wonderful meal and Mehmet was chatty and a good host. I did excuse myself early though, pleading tiredness, and headed for my room.

I decided to get some rest as I intended to wake early and look around.

Friday, November 29, 1991
Lost On My Way to the Kitchen

My watch vibrated on my wrist telling me it was 2.30 am. I chose that time as I seemed to recall reading somewhere that that was the time during which people are in their deepest sleep. I dressed quickly and quietly and put a sock in my pocket ready to put over the camera, thanking all the James Bond books for their ideas. I was relying on luck that no one was watching as I left the room, or at least that they were distracted. At least I could see that there was no light under my door which led to the passageway.

I quietly opened the door and keeping as low as possible left the room. Once out I flattened myself against the far wall and put the sock over the camera. Moving down the passage I headed for the stairs I'd found yesterday. Again I flattened myself against the camera wall and slowly climbed. I'd only climbed ten steps when I felt a turn in the stairs. I followed it round keeping my eyes open for another camera but seeing none. There was enough moonlight to see that instead of continuing up, the stairs started going down again. I thought it very strange as there was nothing here for the stairs to have come to.

Down I went until I reached the bottom. I was on another corridor. There were only two doors. Carefully I opened the first and could hear faint snoring and could see in the dim light the outline of someone on a huge bed at the end of the room. The room looked opulent and I guessed it was Mehmet's.

Shutting the door as quietly as I could, I moved to the second one. This I also opened carefully and could hear breathing. There was a huge gauze curtain in front of me, and pulling it aside I saw a number of beds divided only by more gauze curtains. Each bed was occupied.

Quietly and on tiptoe I made my way across the room looking towards each bed as I went. All the beds bar one had occupants with dark hair. The last one was blonde.

My best guess was that this was Prunella Battersby. To be sure, I gently shook her and as she woke shushed her in case she was alarmed.

“Are you Prunella?” I whispered.

“Yes”, came the reply. “Who are you?”

“I'm David, and I've come to take you home”, I said.

“How touching”, said a voice as the light came on. Turning round I saw Mehmet with Abdullah and one of his armed guards.

“Got lost when I fancied a cup of tea”, I tried vainly. “Just asking this young lady the way to the kitchen”.

Mehmet sneered, turned to Abdullah and said, “Take them both to the cellars”.

Abdullah and the other guard came towards us, and Abdullah gestured that we should follow him and that the guard would bring up the rear.

Passing Mehmet on the way out I said, “This is a very 'short' sighted move on your part, Mehmet. How will you cope when my friends report me missing too? I think their reaction will 'dwarf' any preparations you and your guards will make”.

Mehmet almost snarled but I'm sure a smile played about the lips of Abdullah. We were taken to the cellars and placed in a big room. The door was locked and through the keyhole I could see an armed guard sitting outside.

I asked Prunella how she was and she answered that she was scared but otherwise OK. All the women in the harem had been taken from the nearby villages and held by

Mehmet, yet so far he'd touched none of them. I had a vague notion why this should have been. They were probably held to ensure that the villagers did as they were told. I realised at that point that the harem was a diversion for visitors but a pretence in truth.

I could see that the cellars were actually caves in the hill below the house. I remembered hearing stories that in some crusader forts they had made escape routes in case the Saracens overran the forts. I suggested Prunella try and sleep while I had a look around. Luckily she'd donned a coat over her nightwear while we were still upstairs.

I checked all the walls as carefully as I could. Along the back wall was a row of six huge barrels. They must have been used for wine at one time but whoever had placed them here had made one error. All but one barrel had a wine stain about the tap where wine had spilt. I checked the one without stains, hoping that a bandit fort may have existed here at one time. Sure enough, I found a mark around the front edge of the barrel which indicated to me it that it was removable. I tried and it was. I pulled hard at the front and it came away leaving a large opening to a clear space. I climbed in and kicked at the far end, which fell off with a dull thud. I woke Prunella and sent her through the barrel. I went last so that I could re-attach the front as we left in order to confuse any pursuers. As I emerged on to a sandy cave bottom at the other end, I replaced the end of the barrel. I took Prunella's hand and walked in the direction of a draught I could feel.

Fortunately Mehmet had not ordered us to be searched. I carried my passport, my wallet with tickets and my mobile phone. He probably knew I'd get no signal from inside the cave and hadn't worried. Out here at the cave entrance it was fine.

My first call was to Selim. Rousing him from sleep I asked him to come and get us. I suggested a meeting place just out of sight of the fort.

"Fifteen minutes I be there", he said. I also told him to rouse as many villagers as he could especially those with daughters in the fort. He agreed.

Then I phoned Sir Bertram to say I had Prunella but without a passport. I asked if he could get airport clearance for her to travel.

"No problems, old man", he told me. "If you can get to Sanliurfa airport within two hours I'll have a helicopter waiting for you".

"Marvellous", I told him. "Don't worry, we'll be there".

With my help Prunella managed to get to the meeting place with Selim who had already arrived. There were quite a few villagers there too. Leaving Prunella safely with Selim, I beckoned them to follow and led them back to the cave and its secret. I could hear nothing from the room when I removed the back of the barrel, so I carefully pushed out the front end. Finding no one in the cellar room, I beckoned the men inside. I pointed to the door and mimed to indicate that there was one man with a gun on the other side. One of the villagers spoke some English and confirmed that he had understood my meaning. I knew that the door was locked so I tapped on it. I heard a grunt from the guard and said, "Water, please a glass of water". I heard him move away, but not far, and then return. The key turned in the lock. First the gun came through and I grabbed the barrel and pulled. The guard came inside almost falling and was clubbed unconscious by a villager.

We climbed the stairs to the house and I showed them the harem. I asked the English speaker and one other to follow me. We entered Mehmet's room quietly and as we approached the bed I saw on a nightstand a wig. My suspicions were confirmed, he was really bald and no doubt also a eunuch, which had been my reason for thinking that the girls had been untouched. Mehmet had not wanted his men to know. I wondered whether he had been a castrato as a child to preserve a singing voice and if this had been his revenge on society.

Anyway, I pocketed the wig, and a spare I found on another stand close by. Quietly I indicated that we should leave, though I could see that the men wanted to deal with Mehmet in a different way.

As we left, following the girls and replacing the barrel as it had been, I tried to explain that Mehmet would do no more wrong here. His men would leave when they saw him as he really was, and then the villagers could call in the police and could also help themselves to Mehmet's treasures. They appreciated the idea that with his men gone, no one would be hurt by gunfire and that as well as rescuing the girls they could profit from the night. They sent one man to keep watch to check when the guards left the fort.

I joined Selim and Prunella at the taxi and asked Selim to get us to the airport at Sanliurfa. He did this in a remarkable time and we arrived with our eyes wide and full of fear. I gave him all my U.S. dollars which were probably enough to buy a new taxi and wished him well.

"You good friend, David, you come back we make you Kurd", he said and shook my hand.

The helicopter was there as promised and I helped Prunella aboard.

"Soon be home, old girl", I promised.

"But I can't go like this, David. You simply MUST take me shopping in Istanbul".

I asked the pilot whether Istanbul was our destination and he said that it was. It would be the following day before we could arrange a temporary passport for Prunella and get a commercial flight home. I told Prunella I would help her.

At Istanbul we got off the helicopter and were taken by car to the British Consulate. There we met the diplomatic staff and I was introduced as Lord David which brought a look of surprise to Prunella's face. One of the consulate secretaries gave Prunella a dress that would fit and that she could wear while we shopped and she left to try it on. While she was gone the Consul General quizzed me on what had happened in Sanliurfa in case there were any repercussions for the Consulate. I promised him that there would be none and that the locals up there were probably as pro-British as you could get. He thanked me and handed me an envelope full of U.S. dollars for the shopping trip. Instructions from Whitehall, he said.

Prunella returned and we thanked the consular staff and left to go shopping. I'd been told that two rooms had been booked for us at a hotel so we had a base of operations, as my suitcase full of clothing was also missing.

With so much money, I suggested our first port of call should be breakfast. Prunella agreed and showed me a place she'd visited when she'd been here previously. Though I couldn't have a bacon and egg breakfast, I ate well and enjoyed some Turkish coffee. Then we started a round of shopping. As you will know I don't usually find shopping a daunting task, but today I felt that my legs were inches shorter.

We visited milliners and she bought bras and underwear, asking me to approve every item. She even tried some on and came into the shop modelling it for me. My collar grew tight and I know that there were many disapproving looks from other customers, most of whom were Muslim.

Next came dresses and skirts and blouses. I had to approve every one and have each modelled before me. I thought my face was on fire and just said "Mm, lovely", to everything.

Before shoes and handbags we had lunch. It was a lamb and rice dish that was very pleasant and there was Turkish delight with coffee afterwards. Shoes and handbags were not nearly so stressful, but I did wonder why we needed so much as she surely had clothing back in the U.K.. I chastised myself as this was probably a catharsis for her.

I found a shop where I bought two suitcases for her and a replacement one for me. I was also able to buy two pairs of trousers, two shirts, another waistcoat and a cravat. We still had dollars remaining which surprised me.

At the hotel we had the baggage taken to our rooms which were both nice doubles. We showered, changed and met downstairs at seven as we'd agreed. I'd managed an hour's nap on the bed as well. At seven a very pretty and refreshed young lady met me in the bar and we had a drink before dinner. She seemed very relaxed and engaged me in a lot of conversation. She seemed very attentive to all I had to say in return. I heard all about her life and how she had travelled after being let down by her young man. "I'm sure you wouldn't do that to a woman", she said.

"Certainly not", I replied.

Over dinner the conversation flowed nicely too. She asked me how long I'd been married and whether I was happy. I assured her I was, I mean I am. "These days", she said, "a strong marriage is good. Though I think a little bit of variety injected doesn't go amiss".

Having not thought about that I didn't respond. Eventually we finished and even she had to admit she was tired. We said our good-nights and went off to bed.

As I entered my room the phone rang. It was a Commander Irkun to let me know that Mehmet had been arrested and a vast amount of antiquities recovered. He thanked me for all my help and told me that if I ever returned he would be glad to work with me, but that next time I should notify him that I was there. I accepted the mild slap on the wrist as my due.

I've just finished writing this and am now going to get some sleep.

Saturday, November 30, 1991
Joyous Homecoming

I was woken at two this morning by a movement in my room. Fearing that Mehmet or Abdullah had escaped and found me, I turned the light on. Just in the process of getting into my bed was Prunella.

"What on earth are you doing, Prunella?" I asked, though I have to confess it was a stupid question.

"I'm scared, David", she answered. "I've been in that place for two weeks worried about what was going to happen and I'm just scared he's coming to get me. I just need you to hold me".

"There, there", I said. "He can't get you now. You slip into the bed and I'll lie on top of the covers and hold you till you're asleep. Don't worry, I'll protect you".

A look of annoyance crossed her face as she climbed into the bed. I turned the light off, moved closer to her, and put one arm around her neck so that her head could nestle on my shoulder. She held the hand from that arm with both of hers. I must have started drifting off when I felt my arm move as she pulled it down towards her breasts. I turned a little as though asleep and brought my arm out above her head. To encourage her to sleep, I started to stroke her hair as I used to do when I sat with my daughter.

There was a rather large sigh and she turned on her side. I think she fell asleep soon afterwards if she wasn't already asleep. I, however, didn't go back to sleep and just lay there making plans for when I got home.

At seven I went for a shower making sure I locked the door. When I came back I grabbed fresh clothes and retreated to the bathroom to dress. Fully dressed I woke Prunella carefully and suggested that she went back to her room to shower and dress before breakfast.

She suggested that I went with her to make sure she was safe, but I said I'd check her room before she went in. Everything looked fine and so she got ready and then came back to me so that we could go to breakfast.

The meal over, I asked the desk to arrange a taxi to take us to the airport and requested the bill. I was informed that the bill had already been paid via the consulate. I think some people are remarkably helpful and friendly.

We were taken to the airport in plenty of time for me to buy cigarettes and to get gifts for Lady J and Ysabel. I asked if Prunella needed anything and she went on a minor spree in the airport shops. She came back wreathed in smiles and took my arm.

We had seats together on the plane and not long after takeoff we were served a coffee, after which I dozed off. It was another long flight and so when I woke, Prunella linked arms with me and engaged in chitter chatter.

When we arrived home she was still linking my arm as we picked up a trolley for the cases and headed for customs. We passed through without a problem and out into the concourse, where I looked for Lady J and saw her standing with Sir Bertram. They walked towards us and I found it hard to unlink my arm.

Julia said, “Hello, young lady, don't get too comfortable there”, in a very cheery voice, and then turned to me, and giving me a hug, said, “Welcome home, dear. Another adventure over is it?”

“It is”, I agreed. “ Happy to be home”.

Bertram had given Prunella a hug so I guessed that he knew her and was asking if she were OK. “I'm fine now Uncle Bertie”, she replied. “Thanks to David”.

Bertie grabbed my hand and pumped away at it. “So grateful, old man”, he said. “Never forget this”.

“A pleasure old chap. Looks like we had a good conclusion”.

Lady J and I left to find the car as Bertie and Prunella went off to her homecoming.

“Have you been all right, my dear?” I asked Lady J.

“Yes David, fine thanks, Though we missed you of course”.

“Darling, before I left things seemed a little frosty. Had I upset you or done anything wrong? You know I wouldn't fool with another woman don't you?”

“Of course dear”, she replied. “I'm afraid I was a little cross. It's not you playing with women that worries me, it's them playing with you. You are a little naïve with women you know. They have you tied around their little fingers. I bet that little minx tried to bed you”.

“No my dear, I'm sure she didn't. A well brought up young lady like that? Let’s go and choose something nice for Ysabel's birthday”.

Sunday, December 1, 1991
The Lord and Religion

Well, that was a night I don't want to repeat too often. At 2.15 am I was woken by a 'thud, thud, thud' sound which, as I started to come round, realised was at my bedroom door. I got up to open it just as the cat was making another run at head butting it. He shot past me, the obvious brain damage not letting him realise my door was no longer a barrier. Realisation hit him at about the same time as he hit my wardrobe door, almost splintering it.

At that time of the morning my sympathy level was not at its highest and so I wedged the bedroom door open and headed back to bed. Whilst I'd been wedging the door to prevent a repeat performance later when he needed to leave, he'd made it to the bed and settled in. He was almost squashed as I sat down. We sensed each other's presence at the same time and he reached out a paw tentatively and swiped me. It now looks like I have a bar code on my back. If I ever fall over in the supermarket near the tills, heaven help me, I'll be bagged before I know it.

For the next half hour we remained as master and pet. The master occupied the warm spot in the bed while I remained sitting on the edge, my eyes closing, and almost falling off when I fell asleep.

Eventually he moved over and I swung my legs in, puffed up my pillows and settled down. At 3.15 am he started a route march up and down my body. But, as I was lying on my side, he was on the narrowest bit of me and he had to use crampons to remain in place. There were little pinpricks of blood along my side today.

I was forced to turn over onto my back. There was no choice. Carefully, I did so in such a way that my turning didn't dislodge him all at once. A few walks up and down my front, a few wet noses to my nose and eyes and he finally settled down. It was like a lead weight on my chest. Somehow I managed to get back to sleep again.

I don't know how long I was allowed to sleep, but I came up rapidly from the depths at a tugging sensation on my chin. I realised the weight was still on my chest but it certainly wasn't settled now. He'd decided my beard made a good plaything for him when bored and was swiping at it like a piece of dangling wool, claws extended. I put my hand up at the wrong moment to move the beard and gained striped fingers. I suppose the stripes made them look thinner. In utter desperation I rolled onto my side again, virtually throwing him off in the process. He got the point as he dropped to the floor but he was still able to swagger off.

I slept.

The next thing I knew was a wet nose in my ear. My eyes jerked open in shock and facing the clock I saw that it was ten to five. I realised that I was beaten and should just prepare for duty. I swung my legs out of bed, grabbed my dressing gown and turned to Oscar. “Is it food you want, you rascal?” I asked (actually I won't repeat what I really said), but he was already lying in my vacated bed snoring.

In exasperation I went through to the kitchen to make myself a cup of tea. I was just finishing when Lady J walked in. “Your damned cat”, she said, “kept me up half the night and now he's just woken me again starving to death”. I bit my tongue rather than remind her that 'My damned cat' had been something of a fait accomplis by herself and Ysabel and nothing to do with me. I would happily take responsibility for Joey, but the cat, NO WAY!

I made another drink and we took them through to the lounge. Lady J sat on the settee as usual and after a moment I joined her. The cat was now occupying my chair and there was a malicious smirk on his fast asleep face.

We sat enjoying our drinks in a companionable silence. At 6.30 am I got up and made fresh ones so that Lady J could take her daily calcium tablet. Thereafter would follow four more coffees until the dryness had gone. Personally I think she's just a coffee addict but I knew when silence was golden.

“What would you like to do today, dear?” she asked me.

Not knowing whether this was a trick question and if something had already been decided, I replied, “Whatever you like dear”.

“Typical man”, she said, “I give you the choice and you can't make a decision. Come on! There must be something you want to do”.

“Well, we could always go to a carboot sale”, I chanced.

“No, I think a trip to see Mumu and John would be best”, she rejoined.

I acquiesced.

She went through to shower and dress and I did the same. By 7.30 we were ready to roll. I left a quick note for Ysabel who had spent the night at a friend’s home. We didn't expect her back until early evening, but better safe than sorry.

By 7.45 we were on our way. The journey usually takes a couple of hours as they live out in the wilds. We passed through some beautiful countryside, through forests and past lakes. It's a lovely journey when it's not raining.

Usually on the last stage of the journey, as we pass through a tiny village, I call Mumu to tell her to put the kettle on. They're so isolated that they don't have mains gas so they rely on the bottled variety which seems to take forever to boil a kettle. Today as we dropped down onto the last stretch of road that leads to their house, I asked Julia if she'd like a breakfast at a roadway cafe. I steeled myself for a refusal but she said “That'll be nice dear”, and pulled in.

The interior had been made to look like railway coaches (maybe I should have realised by the name, The Coffee Express), and it was very dimly lit. On the menu were bacon and eggs etc. so I got a clean one (boom boom). In the end we decided on just toast and a coffee each. The toast was fresh and crisp and there were real butter pats to coat the slices in. Handily for me Julia likes the butter spread thin and I like it thick so
I got her spares. The coffee was hot and welcome.

Leaving there, I made my usual call to Mumu saying, “be there in ten minutes, hope loo is free as brother-in-law now needs a wee”. I may not be Rabbie Burns but I do have a poetic side. We were five minutes away from Julia's next coffee when the traffic lights changed to red. Traffic came from the left. There were four lorries carrying biblical themed displays on their platforms, followed by a number of walkers and finally a brass band.

The lights changed to green and we were away again, for all of two hundred yards and suddenly we were at the back of the church parade moving at about four mph. We still had about five miles to go! What seemed like six months later, we were a mile further on and I was starting to hum, 'And when the saints go marching in'. I knew the tune would stay with me all day and probably as badly played as by the band ahead.

Half a mile or so later the parade started turning left. We hurried on with our journey arriving about twenty minutes late.

Mumu answered the door. “I thought you were only five mins away David”, she said.

“Ah, we were, Mumu, but we caught religion on the way”.

Julia had her coffee and I managed to get to the loo. By now it was 10.30 am. John and I would normally have departed to his study but peace seemed to reign between the girls today. We decided instead to sit in the garden awhile. Despite the month it seemed quite pleasant. We sat chatting amongst ourselves for a while when something caught my eye. I turned my head slightly and there on a bush sat a butterfly. "In December?" I thought. I excused myself quickly and dashed through the house to the front where our car was parked. In the glove compartment I keep a camera in case of accidents. I grabbed it and ran back through the house again. Yes, it was still there. I primed the camera and crept forward.

"What is he doing?" I heard Mumu ask Julia.

"I have no idea at all", I heard from Julia.

From John I just heard laughter.

I was close enough now to take the picture. I was about to click when I realised that the butterfly wasn't real. I hesitated, unsure what to do, then carried on forward until I could part the bush, and clicked. "Damn, it's gone", I said.

As I walked back to the chairs John spluttered through his laughter,

"If I'd known, har har, that you wanted to catch my fake butterfly, har har, I'd have brought it over".

"Butterfly?" I said, "what butterfly? I thought I saw a fox trotting across the field and tried to catch it".

"Sorry old man", said John with a smirk twitching his lips. He winked at me and said, "My mistake", earning my eternal gratitude. I knew I'd never live it down if Lady J thought I'd tried to photograph the butterfly as real.

After lunch at a local pub, Lady J and I started home. There were no holdups on the way and being Sunday there was very little traffic about. By late afternoon we were home and within a few minutes Ysabel also arrived. I saw Julia beckon her over as I put the kettle on for a drink, and there was a certain hushed laughter I could just hear over the sound of the boiling water. I carried the drinks through to the lounge on a tray and we all sat down.

Ysabel said, “Daddy, I think I'll cabbage out white here this evening. There's a programme on about a Russian admiral, not that I swallow tales like that any more.” She burst into laughter at that point unable to hold it in any more.

Julia just looked at her and said, “Well David, now we have a new myth about a moth to tease you with”.

Sunday, December 8, 1991
The Birthday

Ysabel's 14th birthday. Hm, I doubt there was any way I could have forgotten it was today as it was just 7.00 am when I first heard the refrains of 'Happy Birthday to ya' by Stevie Wonder blasting out from her room.

Oh Ysabel, subtlety is thy middle name. It's just as well we have no close neighbour to disturb.

I got up and made the morning coffee; I knew Lady J wouldn't sleep through it either. I took her coffee through and she said she'd join me in the lounge in a moment. When she did, we got Ysabel's gifts together ready for breakfast time, which came approximately ten minutes later when Ysabel was sure we were up and about.

"Morning parents mine", she said as she came through. We both greeted her, gave hugs and wished her a Happy Birthday. Though whether she heard us with the deafness her music must have caused is open to question.

First she opened a game which I'd bought for her computer. Sonic the Hedgehog it was called and it delighted her enough to throw her arms round me.

Next she opened clothes, an assortment of jeans, skirts and tops that I knew Julia had chosen under the strict instructions of Ysabel herself who needed to wear the same fashions as her friends to be thought 'cool'.

John and Mumu had sent a gift token which was great as there were always books, records or games she wanted. After opening all her gifts and cards, Ysabel disappeared back upstairs to try on the new things. She came down a little later to show us and to ask if we could eat out. We agreed and set off for Barchester and a little Greek taverna where you were allowed to break plates.

We stepped our way carefully between all the pottery shards to an unoccupied table, and as it was a special occasion, ordered a carafe of wine. While we were waiting we each threw a plate to get into the spirit of things. It looked like an explosion in Staffordshire pottery but was really great fun. That is, it was until 'clunk', something hard, white and ceramic caught the back of my head and I fell forward dazed. The manager rushed over full of apologies. “Zees dinner is onna da house My Lord”, he said.

Another apology came from the parents of the child who had launched the missile. “So terribly sorry”, I heard. “Another bottle of wine, least we can do”, they said.

Slightly less dazed now, I replied, “Don't worry, a plate to the pate won't damage me too badly, but I'd get your son a trial with the county cricket team as a bowler as soon as possible”.

I ordered a meal each for the girls but I no longer felt like eating. I nibbled on a breadstick and tried to ignore the terrible headache that was forming, attempting to get my eyes to focus as I could see two of everything. Luckily I wouldn't be seeing two of the bill. The girls managed to finish their extremely large puddings and we wandered back to the car, one of them on each side of me.

I think I must have dozed off in the car, as the next thing I remember there were bright lights in my eyes and a doctor (or two) standing over me telling me to wake up. I think I heard mention of concussion. That woke me up. Julia and Ysabel were there telling me I'd passed out in the car and only the seat belt had stopped me cracking my head again on the dashboard.

After a couple of hours I was allowed home and I thanked the doctors on one side of me whilst apologising to Ysabel on the other side for spoiling her birthday.

“Please don't apologise Daddy”, she told me. “It wasn't your fault. But I don't want to hear you telling all my friends when they come round that you were caught by a flying saucer”.

I can see that she has so much of her mother in her.

Wednesday, December 25, 1991
Christmas Day

Christmas Day. I love all the traditions associated with Christmas.

I went to bed early last night at about 11.30 pm. I knew I'd be up this morning at about 5.00 am to do my Santa duty and take stockings in to the foot of the beds of Julia and Ysabel. Then I'd put the main presents in the lounge ready for after breakfast.

Tradition in my family has always been that you have to eat some breakfast before being allowed into the lounge to open presents. I'm guessing it was to stop the children of every generation from eating too many sweet things in the run up to Christmas dinner, which in our house has always been served at noon.

So, at 5.00 am I awoke and took the stockings carefully through to the girls rooms - without tripping over the cat - and then put the main gifts as always in the lounge, each bundle of gifts on the chair of the person who usually sat there. The exception was a gift for Ysabel, which just might have dropped off the chair if left alone. I put a little gift on each seat for the cat as he always seemed to think that they were all his.

I'd just finished doing that and gone through to the kitchen to put the kettle on when I heard a bell ringing. It struck me that I'd heard about a tradition peculiar to our village when we'd first moved here.

Every year at about 6.00 am an unknown Santa would start in Upper Greenfield and work his way down to Greenfield Bottom ringing his bell to let the children know it was OK to wake up, Christmas was here. A well loved tradition by all the children of the village if not by the parents, half of whom dashed to get their shotguns loaded with birdshot, swearing they'd get the beggar this year for sure. For the children it kept the spirit of Christmas and their beliefs in Santa alive.

I live in Greenfield Bottom at the end of this mighty run. I heard the tinkling of the bell and saw a flash of red as Santa ran through my garden, then over the fence, across the field and into the door of Owain my neighbour from across the field. If all others had to guess, at least I knew I had seen Santa, and better still, I knew who he was. Lady J and Ysabel missed seeing him come but I knew they'd love to hear I'd seen him.

I made drinks and took a tray through to Julia's room and put it down. Then I crept through to Ysabel's room carefully carrying the cat and deposited him on her feet knowing that he'd pounce the minute her toes twitched. There was an earsplitting scream as Oscar attacked and I almost ran back to the drinks. I had to run as I knew she wouldn't be far behind me and she'd want to wriggle in between Julia and myself. But, if she got there first I'd be left perched on the very edge of the bed. I made it and she got there a close second, her stocking in hand. I passed the drinks out and the ritual began.

"You go first".

"No, you go first".

"Come on Daddy, you start".

I opened the first of my gifts from the stocking which Julia produced from under the edge of her bed. "A new pair of black socks that will play Jingle Bells if I press a button. Wow, thank you Santa", I said.

In turn the girls opened one each, Ysabel a scarf and Julia a book. We went on like this, in turn, until the stockings and our mugs were empty, by which time it was 7.30 am.

I couldn't help but remember my own childhood where at the bottom of the stocking was always a new penny, an apple and a tangerine. I suspect the fruit was there to stop me eating my selection box before breakfast. FAT CHANCE! I'd be eating sweets and reading my Eagle annual right up to breakfast.

"Right", said Lady J with a clap of her hands. "Let's clear this away and have breakfast".

Everything was piled up and put back into the stockings (or Santa sacks) ready for putting away later. The discarded wrapping paper was put into a carrier bag ready for recycling. Ysabel hugged us both and we all headed for the kitchen and the miniature packets of cereal, which was the least we could get away with. Lady J put the oven on (it didn't suit her) and in went a joint of beef ready for dinner. I turned on the radio to try and hide the clunking sound I could hear in the distance.

After breakfast we all trooped into the lounge where there were oohs and ahhs as the girls opened their gifts. When they saw me watching them they made me stop, and start opening my own gifts.

We all got things we wanted and things we didn't know we wanted until that minute. Each of us had one gift left at thc bottom of thc pilc.

Lady J went first and opened hers to find a beautiful gold and opal ring I'd seen her admire recently. She smiled across at me and blew a kiss.

Ysabel opened hers to find a new stereo system for which she'd begged mercilessly for months. She still managed to appear surprised and again we got hugs.

I opened mine to find a new pocket watch with an intricate Celtic design inscribed on the front. I knew that I would want to wear this rather than keep it in my collection. I was a little overcome in truth but said nothing as I hugged them both.

Then I presented Ysabel with the clunk. She unwrapped the box carefully and there inside was a hamster and a ball. "Thelma Louise", she said and promptly lifted it (him) out of the box through which he'd almost chewed and put him in the ball. The clunking sound became more obvious and extreme now as Thelma Louise banged into any furniture that was handy - skirting boards, chair legs, my feet, anything. Then the cat came in and you could see the calculation on his face... Mmmm lunch, prepacked for me.

He pounced, and as he did so, Thelma Louise put on a spurt so that the cat missed completely. He stopped dead in his tracks. Then with a look of disdain he promptly ignored the ball and started attacking all the discarded wrap, jumping in and out of the empty box, as if to say that's what he'd wanted all the time.

After the gift opening was finished we all went to get dressed. Ysabel then drifted off to be with friends until lunchtime. Lady J disappeared to the stables to take her horse the gift-wrapped swede and carrots we'd got, assured that he wouldn't know what they were.

I decided to check my computer messages.

Feeling bloated? asked one. Why not get rid of your Christmas excesses with colonic irrigation? Blimey, I thought, at least let me have some excesses before you ask a question like that. I haven't even eaten my Christmas dinner yet.

Another ad wanted to know if I needed to find God over the holidays. And here was I not even knowing He was lost.

I answered a variety of Happy Christmas messages from friends everywhere, and wished them the same.

At 10.30 am Lady J returned and we sat with a coffee to await our guests.

First to arrive was the Squadron Leader (Lady J's father), whose driving always made me think he was still flying and trying to avoid a Messerschmitt on his tail. He bore gifts of two tins of sweets for us and a large package to give to Ysabel when she returned. We gave him a shirt and jumper in RAF blue which was the only colour he ever seemed to wear.

Ysabel returned soon afterwards and he'd bought her the largest Care Bear I'd ever seen. She'd bought him some ‘Spitfire' cufflinks, and he was absolutely delighted.

Then we heard a roar. Julia and I looked at each other and smiled. Within moments, in through the open front door came Count Fraenkel, a family friend for so long that we considered him family, and treated him that badly too.

“Come and see my new baby”, he said to us, and obligingly we trooped out to view the newest sports car, his pride and joy.

It was really tiny and Julia said “This macro technology is all well and good, but where's the one for your other foot?”

“I'm gonna hit her in a minute”, I heard.

I chipped in with, “You know Michael, I'm told that if you save the original box, toys are so much more valuable”.

Michael scowled and said, “Such Philistines. She's a beauty and I get 56 miles to the gallon”.

“Michael, there's not room to get a gallon in this car - anywhere”, said Julia.

We went back indoors to make him a coffee. He gave Ysabel a new record and she gave her Uncle Michael a huge hug and presented him with a new book by an author he loves.

Julia got a new leather shoulder bag with a horse embossed on it. It was very nice and she loved it. I was given a walking stick he'd found for me which is Japanese from the Meiji period, a work of art.

He opened his gift from us which was a matching Victorian crown, double florin, half crown, florin and a groat all from 1887, which delighted him. I felt sorry I'd not bought him some model cars like the one parked outside.

Lady J disappeared to put the vegetables on and to see to lunch. Michael, the Squadron Leader and I all sat down to chat, while Ysabel went off to play her record. After a while I joined Julia in the kitchen to help carve the joint and put the potatoes and veg in serving dishes while she made the gravy and got the Yorkshire puddings out. “Don't forget to carve WITH the grain”, she told me as though I'd never carved before. I could tell she was nervous.

We called everyone to the dining room and took the food through. We all helped ourselves from the dishes and then pulled crackers so that we could all wear silly hats while we ate. The cat was looking longingly at the food so I went and got a saucer to put a little beef on for him. Impatient as ever, as soon as my back was turned he'd jumped on my chair and grabbed a slice of beef off my plate. I had no choice but to empty the saucer onto my plate. I got the better end of the deal as I'd broken up two slices for him.

Next came the Christmas pudding and brandy sauce, with a reminder from me that there were silver threepenny bits in the pudding and not to choke on them. Then came the gasp for air and the Squadron Leader’s face turned Air Force blue to match his clothes. Every year someone stops listening to me. I went behind him and applied a sudden jerk to his diaphragm. Out shot the blockage, pinged off the light fitting and caught Michael a glancing blow on the forehead. He jumped up without realising he'd tucked the tablecloth into the top of his trousers. The whole of the tablecloth came towards him turning over the brandy sauce jug on the way. He quickly released the cloth and as he did so, the brandy sauce took the opportunity to slide off the now vertical cloth straight onto his shoes.

The Squadron Leader was returning to his normal colour but still trying to force air into his lungs whilst Julia, Ysabel and I burst out laughing.

Michael removed his shoes and socks and went through to the bathroom to wash his feet and wipe the shoes down. I went and got him a pair of the most fluorescent socks I possessed to replace the damp ones.

Bloated, and almost ready to follow the advice on my computer message, I went through to the kitchen to start washing pots while the Squadron Leader, Ysabel and the Count retired through to the lounge. By the time we joined them the cat had taken the only seat left available to me. The Queen's speech came on at 3.00 pm and I intimated I was standing from respect. In truth it was more out of respect for his claws. After his disappointment with the hamster (which he probably thought was his lunch) I wasn't prepared to risk my luck with him.

A little later Julia and I laid out a small cold buffet with my famous beetroot jelly to complement the pickled onions. I'd made a fresh trifle to follow. We'd decided everyone could help themselves when ready and we settled for a game of Trivial Pursuit. The Squadron Leader left at 6.00 pm to start his journey home, and Ysabel went with him to be dropped off at a friend's house. Battle began. We all share a competitive spirit and the race was on to get all our segments in the pie dish. I know absolutely nothing about sport so I knew that my orange segment would be hard to achieve. I thought that if I answered Bobby Charlton to every sport question, sooner or later it had to come up right. I did, it did. Thank you Bobby, you are a prince amongst men. The orange segment was mine and my dish was full. Julia and Michael needed only one slice apiece. Round I went and back again to the centre for my question. Each time, Julia and Michael ganged up and asked a sport question. Round and up again.

"Who won the world cup in 1966?" was the question.

"England!" I cried, waving my arms in the air to celebrate getting possibly the only sport question I could have answered.

"Damn", I heard Michael say, "it's a sport question and I thought the hardest on the card. Sorry Julia".

The day was mine. And though we cleared up soon afterwards and Michael rolled his skate in the direction of home, I went to bed a happy man.

What a wonderful Christmas.

Thursday January 2, 1992
Nightmare in Gay Paree, or How I became the Crow

The phone rang at 8.30 am. I'd been up and about for ages and had taken Lady J her coffee. She was in fact on the point of departing for the stables when she answered it. I knew who it was going to be the moment I heard it ring. No, not second sight, more the way an animal senses bad weather is on the way.

And yes, it was Sir Bertram (Bertie) Threadneedle of HM Government (which department I am only able to guess but I'm sure it ends in a 6). He said he'd be with me at 10.00 am. That gave me time to suggest Ysabel caught a bus into town and visit a friend. I gave her enough money for the two of them to see a film sometime during the day and to have a pizza or some such for lunch. She must have thought it was her birthday again - she did look askance at me.

I'm almost sure that if Bertie thought he was early he'd have parked his car around a convenient corner just so that he could arrive exactly on time. I, on the other hand, had stationed Grizelda on the door and had asked her to start opening it just before he reached it. She brought him through to my study and went to bring in a tray of coffee she'd prepared. In the meantime, Bertie and I made idle chit chat about our respective Christmases, though I had a feeling he probably knew as much about mine as about his own, he was so well informed. Grizelda brought the coffees and we both thanked her. As soon as the door closed the chit chat ceased.

"David, I have a mission for you should you choose to accept it". I waited for him to tell me and then self destruct after 10 seconds. It didn't happen so I asked him to carry on.

“David”, he said, “recently we’ve heard about a plot to assassinate Her Majesty. We know who her assassin was intended to be, but not the where or when. Two days ago this man had an accident in Paris when he went to the dentist. Too much gas during the questions, I'm afraid. We have no idea who hired him. We need you to take his place for a few days and see if you can find out. We must stop this person from getting news of the assassin's death and hiring someone else. His real name was Gilles Legume”.

“If you knew who the assassin was”, I asked, “why was he still out there for hire?”

“No one has ever been able to prove anything”, he answered. “You are roughly the same size and colouring as he was, even a similar age”, Bertie added. “I'm sure you can do this”.

“I'm grateful for your confidence in my ability”, I said without conviction.

He explained that I would need to be in Paris by the following day in case anyone should start to worry about the assassin's absence. It would not be his family as he had none. I would also need to live in his flat until I was contacted again by the contractor or until I found incriminating information in the flat. If I was contacted again, I would need to arrange a face to face meeting so that I could identify him later. This would not be the easiest task as Le Corvin, as the assassin was generally known, did not make a habit of meeting the people who hired him in order to prevent them from identifying him.

I agreed to do my best.

As usual Bertie gave me an open ticket, a large packet of cash and an envelope of notes on the subject to study on my journey. He also told me that anything of value I should happen to find would be mine to keep. He shook my hand and left.

When Lady J returned from the stables at lunchtime, I explained part of my mission and asked her if she'd take me to the airport that very afternoon so that I could make a start.

“Of course my dear”, she replied, “but you must promise to be very careful this time and I shall expect Chanel No 5 from Paris on your return”.

“Naturally, my dear”, I said, and went off to pack. A few minutes later, Julia came to tell me that lunch was ready, pulled everything out of my case and started again - neatly this time.

We enjoyed our lunch of cold meat and pickles with fresh country bread - apart from one incident where I stabbed at a pickle and it got away. It got away to Julia's side of the table, where she took it and ate it with a look of satisfaction. I took the last piece of bread in revenge. Only one raised eyebrow told me she'd noticed.

The run to the airport was fine and I'd left a note with Grizelda to let Ysabel know that I'd be home soon and would bring her a gift.

As Lady J dropped me and said goodbye, I checked my pocket for passport, tickets and cash. Everything was there. I was a little early but that was OK, as I was becoming used to standing around in airports.

I was about to wave to Julia when I noticed that I was in the wrong terminal.

“Julia”, I called, “this is the wrong terminal”.

“Never mind”, she answered through the open window of the car. “The right one is only 15 minutes away, just enough exercise to walk off my round of bread”. So saying, she closed the car window and with a last cheery wave, drove off.

The walk to the right terminal took me only 10 minutes so I still felt as though I'd won part of this round (this round of bread!!).

It was only a short hop to Charles de Gaulle airport. A little French customs officer glanced at my passport. "So, mi lor', you are in la belle France. Pourquoi?"

"Pour plaisir, monsieur", I replied.

"Zut alors", he said, "there is much of plaisir to see. Do you look forward to the one thing?"

The Restoration of the Bourbons sprang to mind but I just replied, "The Louvre, Monsieur".

"Excellent, mi lor', enjoy your stay".

"Merci beaucoup", I responded, just about reaching the end of my schoolboy French.

I gave the taxi driver the address I required and was taken on the worst white knuckle ride of my life, where right of way and consideration for human life were not a priority. Had I been able to, I think my last will and testament would have been written out there and then, but the swaying and swerving of the taxi would have prevented it. Eventually we arrived at the Rue de Poisson, and I just paid up and gave a tip that corresponded with my state of relief.

The flat was only on the first floor, but even so, I took the rickety old lift, as my knees were still knocking from the taxi ride. After what seemed like forever, the lift arrived at the first floor and I was at the door of the flat. Bertie had given me a set of keys and I started to try them. Luckily for me there were only three front door type keys and I got the right one third go. It turned out to be a very spacious flat with two bedrooms all the rooms having very high ceilings. I checked the phone and there were no messages.

One of the keys puzzled me. It looked as though it should fit a safe, and though I guessed professionals would have looked earlier, I decided to search the flat. I was on my second sweep and getting annoyed, when I noticed indentations in the main bedroom carpet from a bedside cabinet, and yet, although the cabinet was still in the room, it occupied a slightly different place. Knowing it could have been removed while cleaning had taken place, and not holding out great hopes, I decided to check. Moving the cabinet to one side, I noticed that the carpet was not tacked down at that point. I lifted it and saw a little square of floorboard.

Picking it up, I found the safe. The key fitted perfectly. Inside the safe was a bundle of money, a small bag of stones which I knew to be uncut diamonds, and a group of paper files together with a little black book, which I guessed did not list his girlfriends.

The cash and the diamonds went into my case to hand to Bertie and the files and book came with me through to the 'salon'. In the kitchen I found a little cream in the fridge that was still within date, so I made myself a coffee to help me concentrate.

The book was full of dates and large figures that meant little to me in the way of events, but I was sure that they indicated when assassinations had been carried out and what payments had been received. Bertie's office would no doubt be able to put names to the dates and would probably be able to trace and recover the fees. The files were different. They contained many details of Her Majesty - size, weight and colouring, together with photographs of her taken with the Royal Protection Squad, and her itinerary for the coming months. I noticed little marks alongside Valentine's Day when she would be attending a special church service. It was very worrying that this information was in the public domain. Or perhaps the details had been provided by someone high-ranking in her service who possessed access to such information.

I'd seen a little boulangerie close by as I'd drawn up in the taxi. I decided to get myself something to eat and take a quick look around the area to familiarise myself with it. I picked up a loaf and some croissants, and while trying to mentally record the details of the area, headed back to the flat.

I had just arrived back when the phone rang. “Allo”, I answered it.

“Le Corvin?” said an English voice. “You sound different”.

“Huh, I still have a toothache”, I replied in my best French accent.

“I wanted to check if you had received my information pack on the subject's movements”.

“I have received them”, I told him, “but dropped some in the bath when I was reading them and may need a little further information”. It sounded pathetic even to me but it was all I could think of.

“What is it you need?” he asked sounding angry.

“Erm, give me a contact number or address and I will let you know when I finish reading if I do require more”.

“I will not give you a contact number, but I have a Post Office Box you can send a letter to”, he said. “But hurry, man”.

“Fine”, I replied taking down the address”, I will be in touch within a few days”. I put the phone down. I'd hoped for a telephone number that Bertie could have easily traced, but perhaps he could check a PO Box as well, though I doubted that the man would have used his real name to open it.

I phoned Bertie and gave him the details but he told me that unless they could actually catch the person going to the box it would be hard, and anyway it was possible that someone else might be sent as a decoy. He said it would be better if I could arrange a meeting, preferably on home ground. I've retired to bed to think about how best to do it.

Friday, January 3, 1992
Fashion Parade

This morning I ate the croissants and then settled to write a note to 'my client', saying that I needed a new list of church services that the subject would attend in the next three months. I also said it would be necessary for me to visit Angleterre to familiarise myself with the ground, so it would be feasible for him to give me the information at the same time if he agreed to meet me. If he were to give me a time and place, then I would make myself free. As I had no name, I just sent it to the PO Box number.

That done, I spent the morning scouring the shops for a suitable gift for Ysabel, finally settling on a scarf with a famous name, which I thought she'd like, and was pleased to find in a small shop on the Rue de la Cochon. I lunched in one of the many street cafés but couldn't bring myself to try les escargots. After lunch I found myself near a shop in which a fashion show was about to start. The windows were curtained, so I had no idea what fashions were to be shown, but it was possible that there might be a nice hat for Lady J. I wandered in and found a seat. There seemed to be no men present and within minutes I could see why. Out came the various models dressed in girdles, bras and all the things that would make my face go beetroot. I stood, intending to make my way out in a hurry, when I was approached by the owner of the salon.

"You see zumzink you like, monsieur? I see you iz ze English".

I guessed that she deduced this fact from my clothing and not from the colour of my face. I stuttered my reply, "It all looks wonderful, madame".

"Would you like to buy zumzink for your wife perhaps?" she asked.

"One of everything in UK size 10", I said, and handed her my cheque book to fill in the amount while I made the excuse of hiding, I mean going to the toilet.

When I returned, the cheque was ready for signing and everything was neatly wrapped in little boxes. I signed the cheque and beat a hasty departure. I heard the salon owner call to my rapidly departing back "Come back soon mi lor'".

I went back to the flat to change as I wanted to spend an evening at the theatre. On checking Ysabel's scarf I could have kicked myself. I had not, as I thought, bought a scarf carrying the name of a god from the Greek Pantheon, but one carrying the name of a viral disease in the UK. (Hermes/Herpes). I knew that I would have to try again on the following day, as I couldn't take that back for her to wear.

I showered and changed, and then changed again. Perhaps an evening watching the cancan was not for the best. Perhaps a good meal was called for instead. I knew that the Hotel Angleterre was not too far away and I'd heard that they served a good meal. In truth, I can now vouch for that. It was an excellent meal and I walked back to the flat feeling replete.

On one of the streets I walked through on my return journey, there were a number of women leaning casually against the walls. I thought it strange that so many should decide to take the evening air at the same time, especially as it felt quite cool.

As I walked past one she spoke to me. "You want some sport, Englishman?" It being late, and I not being the biggest fan of football, which I suspected was on the television, I declined with thanks and walked on. Another, a little further on, asked, "You want a little fun?" to which I replied I was a little tired and again declined. But what a friendly bunch these French women were. So inviting to a stranger. I must remember to tell Lady J.

Back at the flat I realised how tired I was, and so have written this quickly before bed which is where I'm going now.

Saturday, January 4, 1992
A Chance Encounter

First thing this morning the phone rang. It was HIM. My letter had arrived and though he was reluctant to meet me face to face, he would do so, today, in France. I agreed of course and he told me to carry a copy of any British newspaper, folded so that the title would show, and to be at the entrance to Maxim's at 1.00 pm.

I formulated a plan in my head.

I spent most of the morning wandering about, looking for a replacement to Ysabel's infectious scarf. I found a little boutique and was able, between my poor French and their equally poor English, to secure a very chic pair of jeans that they assured me would fit. For some reason they kept winking at me and laughing when I said they were for my daughter. I almost had a fit when they told me the price at the end. I didn't realise that I was buying the building too.

So, after a coffee and a Pernod at a street café, and deciding I didn't actually need a security firm to accompany me and the jeans, I made my way to Maxim's, collecting a paper from a kiosk on the way.

I had decided in my plan to arrive a few minutes early and to keep the paper in my pocket until I should see someone arrive, and to give me the opportunity to look around first. When I arrived it was five to one. I saw a bench nearby and went to sit down so that I could watch Maxim's entrance casually. There was someone else on the bench, and as I looked up, I saw the face of Sir Reginald (Reggie) Dingbat.

"Reggie, old chap", I said, "such a surprise. Are you meeting someone?"

"David, old boy", he replied. "Yes, what a coincidence. No, I'm not meeting anyone. Just relaxing before I see if they have a free table. Are you here to meet someone?"

"Me? Oh no", I said, "just having a break from shopping", and indicated Ysabel's box beside me. "Can I treat you to lunch?"

"Very kind", he replied, "but no. I shall have a very quick lunch and start my own shopping expedition".

By now it was five minutes past the hour and no one else had appeared. I realized that I had my quarry. I excused myself, and turning the corner, I ran back to the flat.

The phone was ringing as I arrived gasping for breath.

"Allo", I said.

"You did not attend our meeting", said the voice that I could now identify.

Thinking quickly I replied, "Non, I did not see you at the doorway, and there were two people sitting close by who seemed to be watching and I was suspicious".

"I was there", he said, "but I met someone I knew and couldn't get away from the fool. I couldn't risk letting him see me meet someone".

My confirmation from his mouth.

"No matter", I told him, "I have now decided when I shall strike so I shall need nothing more".

I put the phone down and rang Bertie. He was frankly amazed when I told him who it was.

"The Comptroller of the Privy Purchases" he said. "We shall arrange to meet him on his return".

Knowing I need not stay in France any longer, I told Bertie I'd also arrange a flight home without delay. He asked if I wouldn't like to stay on a while longer in case any more of Le Corvin's clients should get in touch. “I don't think so”, was my response.

I phoned the airport and found a convenient flight home, packed my case, gathered my parcels, leaving the scarf behind, and locked up the flat. There was a handy taxi just dropping off a passenger which I grabbed and shouted to the driver, “Charles de Gaulle Airport, s'il vous plait”. I sat back, eyes closed for the ride.

At the airport I paid the taxi as best I could with shaking hands, and went inside.

Realising I hadn't got the Chanel No 5 for Lady J, I went to the duty free shop to rectify my error, and picked up a box of chocolates for Grizelda as well.

As the plane started to board, I noticed Reggie amongst the passengers and as (bad) luck would have it, we were seated together. I was tempted to admit to my part in his forthcoming downfall, but instead had to make do with innocuous talk about the weather as we Brits do.

When we landed, I realised that I had not rung Julia to arrange to be collected. That was fortunate, as when we disembarked, Reggie and I were approached by four burly policemen under the direction of Bertie.

“Take them into custody”, he told them pointing at Reggie and me.

“What the…?” I started, but a look from Bertie shut me up. Reggie said nothing at all as we were escorted to two cars parked outside the terminal. All I could think of was that at least I'd avoided customs and paying duty on the jeans.

Reggie was put in one car and I in the other, accompanied by Bertie.

“Sorry about that, David”, he said, “but I thought it would divert suspicion from you being responsible for giving him away if you were arrested as well. This driver has instructions to take you home and I will see you there this evening”. So saying, he got out of my car and entered the one carrying Reggie”.

The drive home was smooth, so unlike the Parisian taxi rides, and my driver joined me for a cup of tea before leaving.

Lady J commented, “You have a strange taxi driver there dear, have you been in trouble again?”

“No my dear”, I told her, “just one of the privileges of rank”. She snorted at that.

I gave Ysabel her jeans and with a delighted squeal and a hug she went to try them on. I gave Grizelda her chocolates and was rewarded with a smile as she disappeared to the kitchen to test them.

That left me with Lady J to whom I gave the perfume and the nicely packed parcels from the fashion show salon.

“Really, David”, she said as she unpacked the parcels, “a girdle! Are you insinuating I've gained weight? And all these frilly items, most unlike you. Did you have a woman out there with you to help?”

“No, my dear, I chose them all myself”, I lied.

She tut-tutted a while longer but gave me a nice hug before going to put them all away.

It was about 6 o’clock when Bertie arrived, and after brief hellos to the girls, he walked with me to the study.

“Well David, he confessed in the end”, he told me as we sat down. “He's been fiddling the accounts for ages, and with a review coming up thought the books would be closed if Her Majesty were dead. He hoped to be home free but now I don't think he'll be free for a while. You did a damned good job, thank you”.

I handed over the cash and the diamonds I'd found. He handed the money back to me, calling it 'my fee', and said that the diamonds would go to the Crown. I wished Her Majesty well of them.

Bertie said his goodbyes 'till the next time' and left.

Feeling rather flush from the 'fee', I suggested a meal out to the girls at which suggestion they both jumped. Ysabel wore her new jeans which fitted well. I don't know if Lady J was wearing her new garments but I could smell the perfume.

We had a delightful meal and got home quite late. As I write this and prepare for bed I wonder if they knew that for a few hours they had been in the company of Le Corvin, one of the most dangerous men in Europe?

Sunday, January 5, 1992
The Quick Trim

Ah, the pleasures of being at home with the family. I wondered what sin I had committed to deserve this.

I got up at seven and made a coffee for myself and one to take through to Lady J.

“Thank you dear”, she said, “I notice that you will need a trim before we go to church”.

Trim? Church? Was I in a parallel universe? “What church, my dear?” I asked. “And are we talking about today because if so my tonsorial surgeon doesn't work on Sundays?”

“Oh, nothing to fret about dear, I have some clippers somewhere. I can do it for you; after all I must have mentioned I used to do it for my father”.

Never! I thought, and certainly you've never done it while we've been married. Though what I actually said, to save an argument was, “Yes dear”.

After breakfast I obligingly sat on a chair in the utility room. Julia draped a towel around my shoulders while Ysabel and the cat arranged themselves comfortably in the doorway to watch the event or to prevent my escape - I'm not sure which.

I heard a click as Julia attached the blade to the clippers while she was talking to Ysabel and asking why she was smiling. I heard the buzz as the clippers were turned on and suddenly found I couldn't swallow.

The clippers touched my head and I felt Julia plough a pathway. My hair felt as though it was being pulled out by the roots.

There was a gasp and I saw Ysabel's eyes slowly widen. The cat just smirked.

“Never mind”, I heard Julia mutter, “soon even it out”.

“Pardon?” I asked, hoping I hadn't heard right.

“Nothing to worry about dear, do sit still”, she said.

The clippers carried on with their task and Ysabel's mouth did not close. I still could not swallow and the cat just chuckled and lay down. I had visions of him rolling on his back and gripping his stomach while laughing uncontrollably.

Finally it was over. Julia brushed my collar and removed the towel. Ysabel disappeared...rapidly.

“What's happened dear?” I asked Julia.

“Just a little hiccup with the grading, dear. I put a grade 2 on thinking it was a grade 4. It'll soon grow back”.

That last statement did it. I ran for the nearest mirror.

“Arrrgh!” I heard myself cry in a strangely high-pitched voice. I looked like an escaped convict. I heard a muffled snigger and saw Ysabel's head around the edge of the bathroom door with her hand held tightly over her mouth.

A HAT! That's the answer, I told myself, and ran, both hands covering the vast expanse of forehead that receded into the distance, to my room.

My top hat will distract people, I thought, putting it on and then using both hands on the brim to pull it back up over my nose from whence it had fallen.

Perhaps a flat cap? No, that just moved around and polished my head to a glossy shine.

At a few minutes before nine we left the house. As the door closed I'm sure I heard the cat laughing out loud. Perhaps I should have worn him as a Davy Crockett hat.

Julia told me we were attending church to show support for the temporary vicar while ours was away on holiday. Because of this my attendance was mandatory and my begging and pleading to remain at home had not borne fruit.

The replacement vicar was the Rev Mistlethwaite. He had called Lady J last week to introduce himself. It occurred to me at this point that had I remained one more day in Paris I'd have been safer.

The church wasn't as crowded as usual, but it wasn't too bad except for the stares I drew as I entered. I'm sure Rev Mistlethwaite was a pleasant man but in villages like ours people tended to stick to those they know.

I can now attest that there was no chance of falling asleep unnoticed during the service. There were so many prayers followed by hymns that I was getting more exercise getting up and down again than an Olympic athlete. And the man was boring. He took longer to read his sermon than it took God to create the world. Still. There was always the hope that my hair would have re-grown before we got out.

Eventually, just before my pension became due, it was over. To the sound of Sally Simms playing the Hallelujah Chorus on the organ we all trooped out.
Amazingly, we were all so polite that we thanked the vicar and said how much we had enjoyed the sermon. It's a British sickness being polite, even apologising when someone bumps into us - such manners.

It was 12.30 and I decided we might as well take a ride into town and have a pub meal. It was nice to sit down to eat even though I was self-conscious about anyone noticing my head. The girls decided to have a roast lamb dinner while I decided on Cumberland sausages on a bed of sweet potato mash and leeks, which sounded really nice. I even ordered a pint of bitter. A young waiter brought the meals over and joked to Ysabel, “How long has he been out of prison then?”, and bless her, she didn't laugh as I hung my head in shame as though I really was a criminal.

As the girls had a pudding I had a coffee and began to feel lighter. Well, I suppose I am much lighter having lost all that hair.

As we left the pub, Lady J announced that we would make a quick detour to the stables so that she could check if the horse's hay net was OK. Though we both like horses, this was not a diversion Ysabel and I welcomed, as Lady J tends to forget time when she is at the stables. Her time is not the same as ours; minutes to her are hours to the rest of us mortals.

Anyway, we arrived and walked over to say our hellos to the horses. I made the mistake of leaning over as we got to the half open stable door. I was adjusting the nameplate on the lower half when the horse stuck his head out and licked my head.

I straightened up rapidly and hit my head on the upper section of the door which was not fully opened. Down I went again, only this time all the way down, totally dazed. Of course the law of happenstance had moved a puddle of water (at least, I hoped it was water) directly beneath my derrière. I could see stars and my right hand was resting in something that a horse's derrière had last seen.

The girls rushed to help me up, but at that moment I was happier on the ground. I heard Ysabel say, “Mummy look, there's blood!” So maybe there wasn't a red mist descending over my eyes. I wasn't too worried as I know the scalp can bleed profusely, and as there's so little flesh stitches aren't often needed.

Out came all the tissues, and bless her, Ysabel was gently dabbing my head and wiping my forehead. As the blood was removed I noticed that Lady J had disappeared. Then I noticed her dashing towards me with a chair from the stable's café. They managed to get me up and into it, though the feeling of putting my wet behind onto the chair was quite uncomfortable. I borrowed a tissue from Ysabel (she wouldn't have wanted it back) to wipe my right hand. I heard someone else approach and, with my head in my hands, could just make out a pair of trousered legs.

"This man been bothering you, My Lady? I see you've put him in his place".

"No no, Masterson, this is His Lordship and he's had an accident".

"Sorry, Your Lordship, I didn't recognise you with that hairstyle. Let me help you to the rest room to wash up".

"Thank you, Masterson", said I, "but I think I may sit here a while longer".

"Nonsense, David", said Lady J, and I could feel the heat of her red face at the haircut remark. "You go with Masterson and clean up while I finish off here".

Groaning, I stood up, only to be nearly knocked down again as Ysabel pushed me to prevent me hitting my head on the same door again. As I was almost upright, the horse licked my head again. A quick vision of a vampire horse drinking my blood flashed across my brain. Masterson led and Ysabel supported me to the rest room, a tiny place with a loo and a sink. Ysabel dampened a couple of paper towels and washed the top of my head that was now tender and contained a blacksmith, a very large hammer and an anvil. Satisfied, she dried me off with another towel which was dry and felt like sandpaper, then led me the few yards to the café for a cup of tea.

"Have you got 50p, Daddy?" she asked. "My purse is at home".

This felt like adding insult to injury as I passed her a pound and she got herself a drink as well. The tea was nice anyway, and someone offered me a couple of aspirins which I accepted gratefully.

Lady J entered and I could feel everyone automatically straighten up and hear the men's heels clicking together.

"Are you all right now, David?" she asked.

"Fine, my dear, though ready to go if you've finished".

"Yes, I've just been waiting for you to finish you tea", she responded.

We drove home and I sat on a newspaper for the journey to protect the seat covers. When we arrived, I decided to have a shower and change my clothes. Julia made a coffee and we relaxed in the lounge. Ysabel went off to do whatever it is teenagers do.

An antiques programme came on the television and the experts were talking of how the barbers of old were sometimes surgeons and would bleed you. I glanced over at Julia whose face didn't move a muscle, though I'm sure she felt my eyes on her.

During the evening, Ysabel joined us and asked what Paris was like, and what I'd seen. I told them all about it. When I was talking about the friendliness of the women on that street near my flat, I saw Julia roll her eyes towards the ceiling and heard her sigh in exasperation.

I don't understand women.

Wednesday, July 15, 1992
Departure and the Birthday Pillow

Julia's birthday. Her 36th though I didn't suppose that that was something I'd better mention. I think 29 was the age she'd settled on and I decided that for the sake of my health, it was the age I'd concentrate on. I certainly ensured my survival by putting Happy 29th on her card, which I just left on the coffee table in the lounge.

Anyway, before all this, I was in bed having a wonderful dream when Oscar decided it was breakfast time, and he would give the job of preparation to me, the most obedient of his servants. He had charged at my bedroom door and as I had left it ajar instead of closing it properly, he had enough power to force a passage. The noise had brought me to the surface of sleep and had penetrated my dream enough for it to appear as a thunderstorm. I came fully awake as I was hit by lightning in the form of Oscar landing on my stomach. My legs stayed where they were but my whole upper body sat upright. I gasped for all the air that had up until that moment sat happily in my lungs. He just edged down a little, sat on my thighs and set up a reverberating purr that sounded like a dentist's drill.

"Food?" I asked. And with a little brrp sound he was off my legs and heading for his bowls.

The clock said 5.30 am. "Oh how I hate you cat. Why is it always me?"

I washed his dishes and fed him, then made myself a coffee and took it through to the lounge. Oscar came through, lay across the chair back and started flicking my hair with a fully clawed paw.

It was at this time that I'd decided to go and get Julia's card and have a little think about her age. I can't understand why women just don't admit how old they are. I've passed 41 and don't care who knows it. Somewhat bored now, Oscar had moved to occupy the settee close to where I'd laid her gifts.

At 7.00 am the postwoman came, and luckily I'd seen her so was able to get to the door as she arrived.

"Mornin', Lord David", she said. "Quite a pile for Her Ladyship today. Is she up yet?"

"Not yet", I replied, "but not long now and I'll wake her with a coffee".

"Well, wish 'er a Happy Birthday for me", she said, and I assured her that I would. She's an asset to the community, our postwoman, as she's often the first to notice a problem in the village, such as uncollected post on the doormat from the day before. She's also a very friendly person.

There were lots of cards and a small box which I also left on the coffee table, and I decided maybe it was time to take a coffee through so that she could open her cards and gifts.

Here was my first mistake of the day.

"David, why are you waking me so early?" she asked.

"Happy Birthday my dear, I thought you'd like to open your cards and put them up".

"Thank you dear", was the response, "but birthdays aren't that important at this age are they?"

"But I thought…", I started, and then realised that independent thought about me being older and still enjoying birthdays might not be appreciated.

"No dear, I suppose not", I said.

"Still, as I'm awake now, I might as well bring my coffee through and have a look", she added.

Back in the lounge I watched her open all her cards with barely concealed glee. She stood all twenty cards up on the mantel and across the window-sills. They looked really good. Just then Ysabel came in. “Morning Daddy, Happy Birthday Mummy”, she said, passing Julia another card. Julia opened it and, chuckling at the humour, put it with the others.

She opened the little box which had arrived and which turned out to be a nice head scarf from a friend in Wiltshire. It was covered in scenes of Wiltshire villages.

Ysabel had bought her a new pair of jodhpurs and I gave her a matching hacking jacket. I knew that her sister had also bought her a pair of riding boots which would be delivered later.

She loved the gifts and after saying her thanks we all went to get dressed.

Ysabel had started the school holidays with a request that we let her stay in France for two weeks as an exchange student. Later a young French boy would be coming to stay in the village in exchange. Today was the day she was due to leave.

Excitement was in her every move and she must have packed, unpacked and repacked her case a dozen times in the last three days to make sure that everything she was taking looked as chic as possible. We made sure she had all her francs ready and they were safely hidden with her passport in a pouch around her waist. She looked like a pregnant kangaroo. At 10.00 am we set off for the school where the teacher supervising the students who would be travelling was waiting. There was a small coach to take them to the airport. She was ready and the coach was ready to leave, so we hugged Ysabel, instructed her to phone when she arrived and waved her away. As the coach passed us I noticed someone had stuck a poster on the back saying, 'Our revenge for 1066'.

The coach now gone, with a last dab of the eye, Julia turned to me and said, "Right. Time to take me to lunch in Barchester. Daddy sent me some cash so I'm going to buy myself some gloves".

"OK", I said, "lead on Macduff".

We arrived at 11.30 am and headed straight for the Barchester Arms Hotel which was close to the shops and also served an excellent meal. Lady J chose a booth to sit in while I went to the bar.

"Two lime and lemonades please", I ordered.

"Sorry, My Lord", came the reply, "we've no lemonade at the moment though the manager has gone to get some if you'd care to wait?"

"Fine and dandy", I said, "we'll sit with the menus for a minute".

I explained to Lady J that there would be a delay with the drinks which would give us chance to see what was on the day's menu.

She liked the sound of the beef stroganoff followed by a strawberry meringue and I chose the stroganoff with a double chocolate fudge gateau and cream to follow. I suspect that this was our equivalent of the jelly and ice cream parties of our childhood.

I got up to go to the bar just as the manager came back bearing a crate of lemonade. He must have caught his toe in the carpet, because the next thing I knew he seemed to have launched himself in my direction. The crate was held out in front of him to avoid dropping it, but it was on a collision course with my midriff and I thought his face was on a collision course with the floor. I found myself backpedalling at the same time as I reached for the crate. It was like trying to make a pass in the game of rugby. My hands gripped either side of the crate as he relinquished his grip. His arms whirled in an effort to regain his balance as he still advanced on me. I reached the end of my backward run as my legs came up against the end of a booth - at least my legs did but my body didn't. I ended up flat on my back in the booth with my head in the lap of a startled lady diner. The crate came to a rest safely on my chest. The manager came to a halt against my legs which dangled over the edge of the booth.

"Well played, sir", he said.

"Sir", said the lady, spoon still halfway to her mouth."Would you kindly remove your head from my lap?" There were little drops of liquid falling from her spoon on to my face as she tried hard not to laugh.

"David", came Lady J's voice. "What on earth are you playing at now?"

"Rugby", I chanced suggesting.

"Please excuse my husband, madam", said Julia to my pillow's owner. "Usually, the second time I take him anywhere it's to apologise for the first time".

My pillow laughed harder and the raindrops of soup continued to fall on to my face. I couldn't help but laugh and said, "I couldn't wait any longer for lunch, dear, and this lady's Brown Windsor soup looked so inviting".

The manager removed the crate, my pillow put her spoon down and Lady J grasped my hands and pulled me upright. I thanked her and turned to apologise to the lady whose lap had saved me and been most comfortable.

"Think nothing of it", she said, "though I'd prefer not to share my pudding this way".

I asked the manager for our drinks and gave the food order, telling him to add my pillow's bill to mine for her trouble. We settled back in our booth.

I removed the fake tan provided by the soup with a couple of tissues and our food and drinks arrived. I saw the pillow go to the counter to pay, and the manager telling her that it was settled. She turned in our direction giving a nod and a large smile. No doubt her afternoon companions would be regaled with stories about her lunch.

Julia and I finished lunch and I settled the bill. The manager repeated his apologies but said it was the best laugh he'd had in a long time. He hoped it had not inconvenienced His Lordship. His Lordship assured him that it hadn't.

We walked along the street to a small milliner's shop which Julia knew and she tried an assortment of gloves. She chose some nice leather ones which I suggested would be perfect for driving. She told me that they would also be perfect for getting a good grip on my neck if need be. Making sure the assistant couldn't see us, I pulled out my tongue.

We had a pleasant afternoon sauntering round the shops getting one or two necessities, some maybe necessities, and, according to Julia, a definitely not necessary corkscrew. I disagreed and said that you could never have too many, to which Julia responded, "You just like new toys, David. Just because they give it a name like The Butler's Friend doesn't make it any better than the last five you bought".

We drove home and I persuaded her to stop once to look at the view.

"Why David?" she asked, "I can almost see this from the house every day".

"Just pretty", I said, not wanting her to realise that I didn't want her to arrive home before 6.00 pm.

It was just past that when we arrived. I let her enter the house first.

A light came on and I heard a shout of "Surprise!", which was followed by a shriek from Lady J. Inside were waiting some of her friends.

Henrietta Fanshaw was there from the Pony Club, Lydia and Carlton Ponsonby-Smythe, Davide and Sybil

Frankel-Ffoulkes, Jenny Thistwell the local teacher and Sally Simms our local organist and celebrity who writes children's books.

The squadron leader had turned up also to help his daughter celebrate.

Lydia rushed over to air kiss me, and to Julia she said, “Happy Buthday, Julia dahling”. Carlton wished her a Happy Birthday then came to shake my hand. “Hello David, old chap”, he said. “Had a good day?”

“Fine thanks, Carlton”, I replied.

“More than fine, you mean", said Julia. "He created a new meaning for the words lap dance today, Carlton. No sooner do I let him out again than he's throwing himself at all the women”.

Monday, October 4, 1993
Sir Bertie and the Indiscreet Letters

Last night was not an easy night. We had offered to keep an eye on a friend's kitten while she was away for a few days. It seemed that the kitten wanted to take advantage of all the facilities on offer during her stay, and of course our cat was happy to be the tour guide.

The tour reached my room at 3:00 am where twin blows to my chest had me pinned down thinking we had burglars. In fact burglars would have been the easier option. I opened my eyes to be confronted by four green eyes watching me very closely. My cat walked up from my chest and stuck his enquiring and cold nose in my face. Seeing my eyes were open he slumped down with one paw on my right cheek and his body wedged just beneath my chin. The other pair of eyes followed suit and lay with one paw on my left cheek, but as she was smaller her body lay across my mouth. Breathing was getting to be harder but screaming for help wasn't an option with just women in the house.

I don't know how long we lay staring at each other but I know that somehow I breathed through it and managed to nod off again. This didn't seem to be part of their plan so both my eyes were assaulted by wet noses in unison. As I woke up again with a start, they turned together in disdain and moved down the bed to settle at my feet. A small sound from Oscar seemed to say, “Not much fun is he?”

By now, of course, I was wide awake and sleep was not on the cards again. All I could do was lie and wiggle my feet under the covers to see if I could annoy the cats into staying awake too. They were both impervious to my teasing and slept on. Eventually I got up in disgust and as I did so, they got up and moved to the spot I'd just vacated and settled down in the warmth.

By 7:00 am I'd taken Lady J her coffee and I'd got Ysabel up for breakfast.

At 8:00 am they were just leaving the house for the stables and school respectively, when I saw the Rolls Royce turn up. Out stepped Sir Bertie. With a gracious bow to the girls, he came inside.

“Morning, old man”, he said. “Lovely day. Ready to resume your service to Her Majesty, I hope?”

“As ever”, I responded. “What problem have you now?”

“David, a member of the Royal Household has been writing what appear to be indiscreet letters to a lady across the pond. She has threatened to publish the letters unless he comes up with a ridiculously large sum of money to get them back. This could become a huge embarrassment to the Royal Family. Already he has been sending money which was supposedly to help with medical expenses, bills and other assorted crises that should have warned him off. We need you to go over and negotiate a smaller sum if you can find her, retrieve the documents and destroy them. I'm afraid the Cousins aren't able to help much as the letters have been going to a Post Office Box and they haven't been able to find her. We know you have the patience for this”.

“Thanks for your faith”, I laughed.

“I have a file in the car for you to read, David. It's a bit sparse as we have no picture of this woman. We'd like you to fly out tomorrow if you could, time is of the essence”.

“That won't be a problem, Bertie, so I hope you have a ticket ready”.

Bertie left the room and brought back from the car a file, a small box, an envelope stuffed with cash, and an open plane ticket. He wished me good hunting and turned to leave at which point Lady J arrived home.

"Hello Bertie", she said. "Where are you sending my husband to enjoy himself this time? I have to decide what's best for him to bring back to those of us left behind".

"Oh, nowhere interesting, Julia", he told her. "The natives all speak English in the United States". With that he gave Julia a peck on the cheek and left.

Grizelda put her head round the door and asked if we'd like a coffee. She disappeared to the kitchen when we both answered, "Yes, please".

"So David, where to and what's in the little box?"

"I don't know about the box, dear, but that can soon be rectified. As for where, until I glance at the file all I know is the same as you. It's America".

"Thank you, Grizelda", offered Julia as the coffee arrived. "We get rid of His Lordship again soon on one of his adventures. Maybe we can get up to some mischief of our own while he's away".

This sounded ominous to me. I sat down with the file and the box that had puzzled us. But no longer, since inside the box, which was small and flat like a cigar box, were ten bearer bonds, each in the sum of ten thousand dollars.

Julia read the file over my shoulder once the shock of the money had worn off. My own cash envelope had about twenty thousand pounds in dollars in it, with a telephone number to ring for more if needed.

The file was thin and the information was sparse. It gave the woman's name as Gloria Peccadillo and the Post Office Box was an address on First Avenue, New York. There was nothing to be done but to fly there and see for myself if I could negotiate a smaller payment or avoid paying altogether.

The airline was kind enough to fit me in for the flight on the following day, so Julia packed me a bag. Her faith in my packing ability seems not to have increased.

We had a quiet lunch of sandwiches at home and then Julia ran me into town where I went to see Freda Newcombe at the library to enquire if she had any maps of New York. She found me a book that broke New York into bite size pieces and showed all the hotels. That done, Julia got into conversation with Freda, and left me to make a few notes from the book at one of the library reading tables. Now that I had some kind of idea of where I would be, I returned the book just in time to hear Julia say, "Wednesday evening then, Freda".

As we left the library I asked what they had been talking about and she answered, "Oh, just a little gathering, David. We're going to sort out a fund raiser and indulge in a glass of wine… or two". I'm never sure why the most seemingly innocent answer can send panic down my spine, but at least I couldn't be volunteered into anything if I wasn't here.

We decided to go to Cass E Dees for a coffee while in town, and were lucky to find a table near the back where we could be unobtrusive, and I could tell Lady J where I'd be staying and could pass on an emergency telephone number. Sherryl the waitress took our order and was soon back with two coffees and two slices of cake. Before I could protest that I hadn't ordered cake, she explained that Simone the owner had sent them, as she put it, free, gratis and for nothing. How very kind I thought.

I tried a bite of cake and could not quite put my finger on the flavour. I asked Lady J what she thought and, breaking off the smallest piece, she found that she could not identify it either. There seemed to be a steady flow of people going past the table to get to the toilets, and each one decided to stop and ask how His Lordship and Her

Ladyship were. I was most gratified by this kindness, but Julia adopted her most suspicious face. My face on the other hand had started to feel uncomfortably warm and the skin seemed tight. Perhaps the heating was on. I took another mouthful of cake but still the flavour eluded me.

Lady J looked up from her plate which she then pushed to one side and asked, "Do you feel all right dear?"

"A little odd actually, my dear", I tried to reply, but found it hard to move my lips. "Come with me", she said, pulling my arm and marching me to the toilet, where, after checking that there were no occupants, she pulled me inside and faced me to the mirror where I saw a man with a red balloon on his shoulders hiding his head. It was a puffy, not very pretty balloon.

"Oh dear", I thought, "I've been poisoned".

"Right". said Lady J. "Doctor's. Now!"

As we were leaving the café, Lady J stopped at the counter where Simone was arguing with another balloon head.

"It's just ground almonds", she was saying.

"Mmph, Mmph", was the response which when translated meant pull the other one it's got bells on.

"Let me look at the packet", said Lady J in a voice to be obeyed. On production she said, "Oh Simone, this is a packet of wallpaper paste with an anti-fungicide. I do hope you're not decorating at home with ground almonds. Please dispose of the rest of the cake before you kill someone and then go and find your glasses".

No one could have been more apologetic as we left the café hurriedly.

Julia bundled me into the car along with the other balloon head and ran us to the surgery. Once there the receptionist took one look at me and sent me along to Dr. Jekyll's room. He took one look and started writing me out a prescription for an antihistamine. I couldn't talk to say thank you but I did write down what had caused the allergic reaction.

“Magic”, he said, “you're the third one so far, so at least now I know what I'm dealing with. Go home, take the tablets and your face should be normal pretty quickly”.

I nodded my thanks and left.

Julia filled the prescription while I hid in the car like a monster. Then we went home where I took a tablet straight away and went to lie down. Sleep must have come because I woke with a start at about 5:00 pm when Ysabel knocked on my door and came to see if I was OK.

“Poor Daddy, in the wars again I see”, she said. “Fancy a nice cup of tea?” Checking that my mouth felt loose enough to drink it, I raised a thumb and nodded. In the lounge, Julia told me that Simone had sent a letter of apology and there was a large cake in the kitchen. She said she'd understand if I wanted to take action but that she hoped not to lose our custom.

Simone's cakes have a well deserved reputation for excellence and as this was a genuine accident I had no doubt that Lady J would have put Simone's mind at rest. I also had no doubt that the story of how my face looked would be stored, improved upon and saved for the future.

It was obvious that I wouldn't be the best company in the world that evening, so I decided to turn in early in preparation for the following day’s long haul flight.

Tuesday, October 5, 1993
The Subtle Taxi Driver

We had an early start for the airport in the morning. I had offered to go by taxi but Lady J wouldn't hear of it. By 5:00 am we were on our well-trodden route to the airport. By 6:30 am I was hugging her goodbye as my face was still a little swollen and a little tender, making a goodbye kiss difficult.

Check-in was fine, though I did draw some funny looks and one girl who spotted me pointed in my direction and burst into tears. She looked to be about twenty, so I hoped it was empathy and not fear that brought on the tears. Of course she might just have had a very bad engagement to a red lollipop.

I picked up some duty-free cigarettes in the shop and then went for a coffee so that I could take an antihistamine. When we boarded the plane, the flight was long and tedious, especially as Dr Jekyll had advised no alcohol while taking the tablets. I guessed I wouldn't get away with asking about the period in between the doses. Luckily the in-flight movie was so bad that I was able to sleep a bit.

My arrival at New York was on time but my departure from the airport was a little delayed while my passport picture and my face were compared, accompanied by a few sniggers. The passport control officer kept calling people over to make a point of showing my face to most of New York for their entertainment. My face must by then have been lollipop-coloured as well as lollipop-shaped. Eventually there was no one left to show it to and they let me through. I got a yellow cab and asked for the Crown Regent Hotel. The taxi driver kept looking in his rear view mirror at me but kindly said nothing. When we reached the hotel he took my bags to the door and said, “Strewth, pal, I'm sorry about your face. A bad fire was it?” I just grunted and passed over his fare with a good tip.

A concierge took my bags to reception and then to my room after I had booked in. I passed over a $10 bill and closed the door behind him before he could speak. It was 8:00 pm and I was not yet ready for sleep, my body clock having been thrown out by the flight. I went down to the restaurant and had dinner, choosing to sit in a dimly lit booth to avoid any comments. The meal was pleasant and I had a bottle of beer with it as I couldn't see what harm it could do. I signed the chit to charge it to my room and then headed up there in the hope of getting some sleep before the following day’s search for the blackmailer.

Wednesday, October 6, 1993
If I Told You I'd Have to Kill You

I did manage to get some sleep during the night but still felt a little fuzzy this morning when I woke at 6:00 am NY time. Not having any idea how long it would take me to find the Post Office Boxes and also a place from which to observe, I decided a good breakfast was in order.

The restaurant dining room was quite crowded but I saw a table with just one occupant. I walked over and asked the lady if I could join her. She indicated I could sit down which I did with a nod of thanks and picked up a menu. The full English breakfast looked good so I ordered that with some fruit juice and a pot of tea. When the juice arrived I took a tablet and put the box on the table.

"Jessie Trenton", said my table mate, "it's nice not to have to eat alone".

I wasn't sure about her definition of eat as all I could see in front of her was a bowl of sawdust.

"David", I responded, offering my hand to shake. "I'm glad of the company".

My breakfast came and I saw the definition of a 'full English breakfast' was a little overstated as my plate alone would have fed Nicaragua for a week.

Partway through the meal and the small talk that we indulged in, Jessie told me, "Well, I have to go now but it would be nice if we were able to eat together again if you're here for a few days".

I responded that the idea sounded pleasant and she wished me goodbye for the present. As she left, I notice my tablets were missing from the table, and I called her back. "Jessie, I think you've picked up my tablets by mistake".

“Oh, I'm so sorry”, she said, “I thought they were mine. Here they are”, she said pulling them from her handbag and putting them on the table. “Until later, then”, she said.

She had left the dining room before I noticed that they weren't my tablets she'd left me but her own. The box was similar so I could understand the mistake, but I was sure that New York did not hold such dangers for me that I'd be needing birth control pills any time soon.

After breakfast, I took a cab to the block where the Post Office Box was and looked around the area. There was a diner over the street but I didn't want to rouse any suspicions by sitting there for too long. I entered the building where the PO Box was and found it to be very open and no place from which to watch the box easily. There was a seedy-looking man at the counter and I took a chance on making a suggestion to him.

“Let me get this right, bub, you're willing to pay me $200 to let you work here cleaning the floor. No questions asked”.

“That's right”, I answered. “I need to check if my wife comes in to collect mail”, a lie of course but the best I could do at short notice.

“You're hired”, he answered.

I'd seen a store close by and so I went and bought some overalls, a bucket, mop and brush then returned to start my employment. I alternated between brushing and mopping the floors for four hours before someone came in. I was about to ignore the movement because it was a male, when I noticed he had opened a box near to the one I was observing, possibly even the very same one. When he'd gone, I went over to see if I could identify the box he’d opened as the one I had been watching, but I just couldn't be sure. I worked another couple of hours but no one else approached the boxes at all. It occurred to me that a man could easily open a box for someone else. I asked Seedy Man if it was a man or woman who usually collected from the box I was interested in. $200 loosened his scruples about privacy and he admitted it was the man who'd been in earlier. I thanked him and packed up for the day.

For the afternoon, I went on a guided tour of NY in different taxis. My favourite place was the Empire State Building where the wonderful art deco designs fascinated me. I returned to the hotel in time for dinner and was grateful to meet Jessie on her way to the dining room as well.

“I'm so sorry, Your Highness”, she said. “I gave the wrong tablets to you this morning”.

Laughing, I responded, “I'm not a Highness, Jessie. If you want to be formal I'm My Lord but I'd prefer it to be David. However, here are your tablets. My reputation is intact so I've not needed to take them. I hope you've not been forced to rely on my tablets?”

Jessie returned my antihistamine tablets with a laugh and said, “Since the pollen count is low, I've not been forced to use yours either”.

We went into dinner together, and after we'd ordered, Jessie told me she was an advertising executive here in NY, and was trying to convince a new client to sign up with her agency. He was a toy manufacturer and she had a couple of days to show him that it would be to his advantage to sign with her to advertise his new line of toy guns.

“Ha ha”, I laughed”. You should do an ad with a spy like James Bond pretending to break into a factory to steal the latest technology in guns because his own office won't buy him one. In the never ending fight for democracy, only the best is good enough”.

“That's genius”, she said, “just the kind of thing I want. What do you do, David?”

“Oh, if I told you that, Jessie, I'd have to kill you”. I answered laughing. “Really I just correct mistakes”.

We both enjoyed the meal and I found her company quite stimulating. Afterwards she asked if I'd like to go dancing, but I had to refuse. I'm not much of a dancer and I wanted to phone Lady J before it got too late.

Back in my room I made the call and checked that everyone at home was OK. I was hearing the news when there was a knock at the door. I told Julia I wouldn't be a moment and went to answer. Jessie stood there with a bottle. I indicated that she should sit down as I was on the phone. I continued my conversation with Julia, and she asked me who'd been at the door. I told her it was a friend dropping in for a nightcap. “Male or female?” she asked.

I answered that it was a female. “Oh David, and you've let her in? You are so naïve sometimes, dear”. With that she put the phone down.

A little shocked, I turned and there was Jessie holding two glasses of wine. She was in a coat but it was open to reveal a shortie nightie underneath. I thought how pretty it was, and wondered if she'd changed because she was tired and ready for bed.

“I'm so sorry, Jessie”, I said,” I can't drink at the moment because of these tablets. Was there anything special you wanted?”

“No, I just thought two strangers in New York could give each other a bit of company”.

“How nice”, I said, “would you like to talk or shall I see if there's anything on TV?”

We did talk, and pulling up another chair, I heard all about her life in South Carolina as a child, marriage, divorce and then a new start on her own. I must have responded the right way because at about 2:30 she gave me a huge smile and said, “Well David, perhaps I should go back to my own room now. I'm tired, a little drunk and you've been a perfect gentleman".

She left and I was able to get some sleep.

Thursday, October 7, 1993
The Heir Hunter

Jessie wasn't at breakfast in the morning but that was perhaps due to the wine the night before. I ate quickly, had a couple of cups of tea, and left to start work.

It was about 10.00 am when the man came in again to check the box. I was brushing the floor and it looked as though he hadn't noticed me after his first glance. It's funny how some people in certain jobs are just taken for granted. As he started to leave, I dropped my overalls to the floor and put them and the brush behind the counter, then prepared to follow him.

Seedy Man asked, "What do you think you're doing? You can't drop everything in the middle of the day and leave! What do you think I'm paying you for?"

"Actually", I said, "It's me paying you, remember? And I have things to do".

"You can't get good staff any more", I heard him say quietly as I opened the door and left. I could see my quarry about a hundred yards ahead on my left and started to follow him. It was just as well he was on foot, but then I'd expected he would go to a local office.

After two blocks he turned into a nice building that was divided into flats. By the time I got there the door had closed again. I noted from the nameplates that there were four flats, two occupied by men and two by women. I had no idea which of the women he was taking the mail to.

I was wondering what to do next when the door opened and a man came out. It wasn't my quarry so I caught the door before it closed behind him and went in. None of the names on the flats had said G. Peccadillo but as there were only two women, it seemed that she shouldn't be hard to find.

I rang at the first woman's door. There was no answer so I knew that G Peccadillo wasn't Renee Stompanato. I rang at the bell of Jeannie Hertz but there was no answer from there either, so I ruled her out. Now I was stumped until I realised that she must live either in the flat of Mr P. Revere or that of Mr D. Joly. And one of those two had already left.

I approached the two remaining flats. From one I could hear absolutely nothing. From the other I could hear what sounded like a radio. It had to be this flat and she must be staying with P. Revere, and therefore it must have been he whom I followed back from the Post Box building.

I knocked at the door and my man answered it. "Yes?" he said.

"Mr Revere", I answered, "I'm Donald Blumenthal from 'Eagle Heir Hunters'. A Mr Reginald Revere died intestate and I'm trying to trace heirs to the estate so that it can be divided up rather than going to the government. May I come in and ask you a few questions?"

No normal person would pass up the chance to inherit money and right on cue his first question came. "How much?" he asked.

"Well the estate's worth about $100,000.00", I lied, "but as yet we don't know how many heirs there are. Actually NONE have been found yet".

"Come in, come in", he said, "take a seat, would you like a coffee?"

"That would be lovely, thank you", I said.

Mr. P. Revere went off towards his kitchen. I noticed some letters lying on his open bureau and risked a look. Some were addressed to Gloria Peccadillo and some to a Paula Tennant. I also noticed as I moved to sit down again that a picture on the wall by the bureau was askew and the carpet on the floor below had a rumpled look as though someone had pushed the edge as they moved away quickly. I'd seen this kind of clue before at home when Lady J was searching for my cigarettes and didn't want to get caught looking. I now assumed that there was a safe hidden behind the picture, and guessed that our Mr P. Revere was in fact the woman threatening to embarrass the throne.

He returned with the coffee and I sat down in plenty of time. He answered all the questions I could invent about the deceased Reginald Revere and his tie to the family, which I'd had to bias in his direction to keep him dangling. I took my leave saying that I'd be in touch and that things looked promising.

Back at the hotel I started formulating a scheme to relieve Mr Revere of the letters I wanted, and I didn't intend to pay for them either unless I had to. After a while, I realised I was hungry and that it was time for dinner. I hadn't noticed that time had passed by so quickly.

Jessie was at her table so I meandered over to say hello.

"Hello, David", she said. "Sit, join me. I wanted to apologise for last night".

"What, for giving me your company?" I asked, not wanting to embarrass her for getting a little drunk. "No need to apologise. It was a kind gesture on your part to a stranger, and I appreciate it".

"I hope you don't think I do that all the time", she said.

"Not at all", said I, "I'm sure not everyone is welcomed to the city by so charming a lady".

All mention of the wine now dismissed, we ordered our meals and settled down to eat. As the meal ended, Jessie announced that she was retiring to her room to read, but said that if I needed company later I would be quite welcome to go along, no strings attached. I'm not sure why she added that, but I thanked her and said that I'd probably be getting an early night. For some reason, she kind of rolled her eyes at that and then sighed. I wish I knew what I'd done wrong.

Friday, October 8, 1993
Cold Packs for the Pain

Up bright and early and down for breakfast by 8:00 am. Still had not formulated a plan of action.

I was taking a taxi to Seedy Man's establishment when there was an accident. We came to a very sudden halt. My body slid back in the seat and my head jerked forward. Then my body moved forward again and my groin came to a quick stop against the head of my walking cane. The pain was instant and excruciating and then my head snapped back hurting my neck. The taxi driver was so worried that he called an ambulance which took me to hospital.

On reaching there we realised that my spherical orbs had swollen to elephantine dimensions. I needed cold packs, and for the whiplash I was given a collar. The nurse on the ward kindly asked if anyone needed to be informed as I would be kept in overnight at least. I thanked her and asked her to ring Lady J so that she wouldn't worry. I asked, "Please only mention the whiplash to avoid any embarrassment."

As my nether pains receded slightly with the cold packs, I was able to sit up and after a hospital dinner in the evening I was able to get to a phone and I called home.

"Hello, my dear. How are you?" she asked.

"Oh, just a little stiff my dear", I answered, flummoxed as I heard gusts of laughter down the phone from Lady J.

"Not too much damage, then", she said as I realised that the nurse had told all. Julia was referring to the worst of the damage and I was referring to the whiplash. Sometime I think the gods conspire to make me look a fool.

Saturday, October 9, 1993
The Superb Play

I was woken at 6.00 am and given the gift of pain relief. I found I that could walk without doing a John Wayne impression and that the swelling had gone down a great deal after the overnight application of cold packs. I was therefore grateful after breakfast to be released.

During my wakeful hours in bed, I had semi decided on a strategy with reference to Mr Revere and the letters. I decided I needed to be a bit more nimble to get away with it, and resolved that Monday would be action day. In the meantime I would make the best of my New York stay. Back at the hotel, I asked the desk clerk to arrange a ticket at a theatre that evening. I chose a play by Gary Morgenstein, who, I was told was an up and coming playwright/director.

This afternoon after a light lunch at a pizzeria I spent some time hobbling around Bloomingdale's before returning to the hotel laden with gifts to take home. I was pleased because I'd found a nice tiepin for Bertie showing two hands clasped. On the back of one was a Union Jack and on the back of the other were the Stars and Stripes.

Dinner tonight was different. I had a small piece of alligator in a beer batter as a starter, followed by a steak with fries and a side salad, with a key lime pie to follow. After I'd had a coffee I was replete. By the time I'd seen a magnificent show and congratulated the author I was ready to sleep, and nearly did so in the back of the taxi taking me back to the hotel.

On my return, I turned in straight away.

Sunday, October 10, 1993
A Walk in the Park

I saw Jessie at breakfast. She looked a little uncomfortable as I sat down, but soon there was a smile directed at me as I said I'd looked for her yesterday and had missed her company at dinner.

"I'm afraid I was out and about shopping", she told me.

"No matter", I said. "Perhaps you have a little free time today for a walk in Central Park?"

"I'd love to, Lord David. And I'd also be glad of the chance of a chat", she said. A little intrigued, I arranged to meet Jessie in the lobby at 10.30 and was promised the chance of a real hotdog in the park.

The weather was crisp but the sun was shining as we entered the park. Jessie linked her right arm to my left and with a tap of my cane we started along the path. I was still walking a little gingerly. Jessie told me I was looking better and walking easier now. She hoped that I felt OK.

I promised her that I did.

Trying to prepare myself for the following day, I asked Jessie if there was a community of actors in New York. She looked at me a little oddly but said that yes, there was a well known school of performing arts and that there would be actors aplenty there.

"Time to stop for a rest and a little chat", she said.

"Fine", I answered, "I see a coffee vendor over there, let's grab one and sit on a bench for a while".

I bought two coffees and we sat down.

"David", she said, "I have a small confession to make".

"Would it be that you belong to one of the agencies and that our meeting wasn't entirely accidental?" I asked.

"How on earth did you know that? Have I slipped up somewhere?"

"Not really, Jessie. But to suggest that I was looking and walking better is to suggest that I told you about my accident. As I know that I didn't, I can only assume that you found out another way as the hotel doesn't know. Also, I just asked you about the actors and you showed no curiosity, so I'm guessing that you already know why I need one. Lastly, you called me Lord David earlier, and how can you possibly have known that?"

"How silly of me", she said. "David, I'm Special Agent Trenton of the FBI. I was assigned to protect you if I can and to help you get your letters back. Though this is a matter of a foreign national and the CIA would normally have dealt with it, it was decided that as we have better jurisdiction in local areas it would be the FBI's responsibility".

"Well, I'm delighted to meet you, Special Agent Trenton. If all agents are as pretty and as good company as you, then no one could complain at your help".

Jessie asked what I'd managed to find out, and when she heard that the crook was a man, she said that it was no wonder they hadn't been able to find a woman when Bertie's department had approached for help.

She asked what I intended to do and I explained my plan with an actor.

"Very good plan", she told me, "but I think I know an agent we can use for this".

"We?" I asked.

"Certainly 'we'", she answered. "Now we know where the letters are, we can get them back, and any others that are there. And, if any of the other victims will offer to testify to blackmail, then Revere will be going away for long enough not to upset anybody else".

We agreed to have dinner together and then meet in my room, and would bring the other agent along as well. In the meantime, we had gone out to have a nice walk and a hotdog, so for the moment, it would be pleasant to concentrate on that. The hotdog was surprisingly good with lashings of onions. It was much larger than I expected. After that we strolled arm in arm back to the hotel where, with a little peck on the cheek, Jessie went off to make her arrangements with her headquarters.

Dinner was a nice affair. All of my recent afflictions seemed to have gone and Jessie was full of banter. After coffee, we went up to my room and found our co-conspirator and my safety net waiting at the door.

"David – Chuck, Chuck – David", said Jessie by way of introduction, "Shall we go in and intrigue, gentlemen?"

I opened the door and we each found a seat. I called to room service for coffee and also for sandwiches for Chuck who said he'd come straight from another job. We intrigued for some time and then Jessie took Chuck away so that I could sleep.

Monday, October 11, 1993
A Royal Blush

I went down to breakfast at 8.00 am and was surprised to find Jessie and Chuck there together already. I joined them and ordered coffee and toast.

"Just toast, My Lord? That's no way to start the day", said Chuck.

"I think David has a touch of nerves, Chuck, he's not a professional like us".

"Really?" said Chuck. "He certainly plans like one".

"Oh he can plan", said Jessie, "but I wonder if he can adapt as we have to".

"Have you two forgotten I'm here and aware of this conversation?" I asked to laughter from them both. We arranged to meet up again at 10:00 am at Revere's building after I'd phoned to check he'd be there.

Dead on time I arrived and pushed his bell. He buzzed me in and I climbed up to his floor to find Jessie and Chuck had arrived early and were out of sight around the corner from his front door. Chuck passed me a small box I'd asked for and I tapped on Revere's door. He must have been waiting as it opened almost immediately.

"Good morning, Mr. Revere", I said as I entered the flat. "Just a couple of things and I won't keep you long".

"That's OK, Mr Blumenthal", he said, "I'm just looking forward to hearing more about Uncle Reggie".

We sat down and I declined his offer of coffee, suggesting that we got down to business. I asked Revere if he had a passport.

He answered that he had and that it was in his safe.

“Good”, I said and asked if I could see it to verify who he was. I was very relieved at this point that he'd answered as I'd hoped. I waited until he'd reached the safe behind the picture and had dialled the combination. Just as he was opening the safe door and putting his hand inside, my own hand went deep into my pocket to the box Chuck had given me. I pushed a button.

Immediately came a heavy pounding at the door. Both Revere and I looked startled though mine was an act. He started to close the safe door and I said “No rush, Mr. Revere, I'll wait if you want to answer your door”. He looked at me, stopped closing the safe then went to answer his door.

As he left the room I ran quietly over to the safe, opened the door and gave a sigh of relief that my guesswork had proven to be correct. There were bundles of letters held together with elastic bands. I grabbed them all and started to disperse them about my person. I put the safe door back to the position I'd found it. At this point I could hear raised voices in the hallway, I stuck my head out.

“Hey man, why is you prettenin to be me?” I heard. “I is Paul Revere wit de Uncle Reggie. You ain't”.

That was my cue from Chuck.

“What, another Paul Revere? Come with me while I check you out”, I said and started pushing Chuck before me. “Thank you Mr. Revere, I'll be back to see your passport as soon as I've sorted this out”.

We moved quickly away from the door, picking up Jessie on the way. We ran downstairs and out of the door and piled into Jessie's car which was parked conveniently close. We pulled into a coffee house not too far away and settled into a booth. We were all smiling at our success. With steaming coffees in front of us, I pulled all the bundles of letters from my pockets. As before, some of the letters were addressed to Gloria Peccadillo. I took those to sort, and shared the others, addressed to Paula Tennant, between Jessie and Chuck. It didn't take too long to find my bundle, nor did it take much reading to see why they might be an embarrassment to the Royal Family. Even reading some of the things made me blush. Putting the offending bundle in my pocket, I passed the remainder of the bundles relating to Gloria Peccadillo over to Jessie. " I know you'll let me know if anything involving British subjects crops up". I said. "Have you found anything of interest yourself?"

"Yes indeed, David, there are a couple of leading manufacturers here, as well as one chemist on the government's payroll. Heaven only knows who the rest are. But, be assured we will find out and then they can rest assured that he won't be bothering them again. May I see the ones you rescued?"

"I'm afraid not", I answered, "I promised my client confidentiality, and I'm sure your government extracted the same promise from you".

"Fair enough, David. Forget we asked", said Chuck. "OK to drop you back at the hotel now so that we can take these to HQ?"

"Wonderful", I said, "I'd be much obliged".

As we pulled up at the hotel I thanked them both for their help, and got out. I was surprised when Jessie also got out. She gave me a hug and whispered, "What could have been, David, if only you'd been less honourable. I didn't come up to your room as part of my job".

I hadn't time to ask her what she meant before she was back in the car and away again. Oh well, if I'm ever here again perhaps I can ask her. Ladies have a language I just don't understand.

Inside the hotel I phoned to see if there was a flight available and was told that there was one leaving in three hours. I gave them my ticket number to confirm a seat, and then asked the hotel to make up my bill while I went and packed my bag.

I went down and paid my very reasonable bill, and within ten minutes was in a yellow cab on my way back to the airport. I listened to the driver's chatter and agreed that New York was great and that I'd love to come back.

At the airport I rang Julia, knowing it was 8:00 pm at home. She seemed delighted that I was coming home and promised to meet me.

A very long and again tedious journey and I was home. I whizzed through customs and there was Julia to meet me. We hugged and then with my luggage deposited safely in the boot we set off.

As she drove, she told me of all the things that had happened while I had been away. No one had actually sued Simone over the cake incident, but at the moment her cakes weren't selling too well. Lady J had just advised her to have a day where the cake was free, followed by a few days at half price to convince everyone that all was normal. Simone had also found her glasses and got herself a spare pair.

It was quite late when we got in and I was tired, so I left my case unopened and went to bed. The girls would have to wait until the following day for their gifts.

Night all.

Tuesday, October 12, 1993
Hitting the Jackpot at Home

Oscar welcomed me home. As I got up to go to the loo in the night, he rubbed against my ankles and tripped me up. I landed belly down in the saddle of the rocking horse in the hall. No doubt wondering why I'd come to such a sudden halt, he jumped up onto my back. From my point of view it felt like he was doing a victory dance up there or perhaps just surveying his domain from a new perspective. I was most definitely a serf under this master.

Gingerly I raised myself off the horse. As I did so, Oscar moved slowly up my back, using his claws freely until he attained an upright position on my shoulder. In the best parrot fashion he sneezed in my ear.

He sat there until I got back to my bedroom and then jumped on to the bed. As I slid under the covers, he moved onto my chest, lay down and purred. The sound was deep and loud. For ten minutes I scratched his head, and then feeling wide awake I gently extricated myself and went for a coffee.

As it was only 6:30 am I had time to enjoy it before making one for Lady J. I called to Ysabel to get up and heard her whoop with delight. I got the gifts from my bag and took them through to the lounge.

Lady J emerged first with her coffee in hand and I passed her a large bottle of perfume and a silk scarf which I knew to be exclusive. She loved them and I earned my first hug of the day. Ysabel came in and seemed very excited with the jeans and jumper from Bloomingdale's which she described as awesome, and was even more pleased with the Bloomingdale's bag itself. By 8:00 am she was dressed in them and off to school.

Lady J returned from dropping her off and said she wouldn't be going to the stables today. I felt honoured, though she did say she fully expected me to take her out. I reminded her that I'd have to check if Bertie was coming and she replied, "Fine, dear".

Not only was Bertie coming but he arrived before I'd finished the call to his office. He must have contacts everywhere to for him to know that I was home again.

"Wonderful to see you, David", he said as he came in. "Did you have any joy?" That question at least proved to me that his people didn't know everything. I passed him the letters and said that I'd leave the decision to him as to whether they were destroyed or kept to remind the individual who wrote them to be more careful. I then passed him the box containing the bearer bonds. He looked surprised. "I managed to get hold of these", I told him. "I saw no good in letting the blackmailer profit from the author's stupidity". I then passed him the little tie pin I'd bought and he looked touched.

"David, thank you, it's wonderful. I take my hat off to you. You have unplumbed depths haven't you? Constantly surprising me. Now, let's hear the story".

So I told him and Lady J the whole tale, minus the accident which I didn't think was relevant.

"Amazing", said Bertie. "You even got the Cousins to co-operate and now they owe us a favour".

"Well done, David", said Lady J, "it shows you have the BALLS to do anything". I flinched!

When Bertie had gone, I took Grizelda a box of chocolates that I'd bought her in New York and told her that we'd be out for meals today.

We drove up to town to have a coffee at Cass E Dees to show that there were no hard feelings and then we took a walk around the shops and picked up a jumper for Julia to wear with her new scarf.

As 4.00 pm approached, we drove to Ysabel's school to pick her up. Offering her the chance to eat dinner wherever she liked in her new finery, she squealed “Fernando's”, which is the new 'in' place out on the Denton Road. As it was only about half an hour’s drive away, we agreed with the choice and made our way there. When we arrived, the car park was quite full in line with its reputation. A sign on the attached pub, 'Hideaway', said that they didn't open until 6:00 pm so I realised that Fernando's was definitely the draw for all the cars.

As we went in, the maitre d’ approached to ask how many there were in our party. On hearing and seeing three, he beckoned us towards a table. We saw acquaintances as we passed other tables and waved or nodded politely. Our table was set for four people and was tucked in a little booth at the rear of the room. Menus were quickly brought to us and without doubt there were some good choices. I ordered some soft drinks while we chose our meals.

When the drinks arrived, we had made our decision. Ysabel ordered an individual pizza with vine tomatoes, Parma ham, mozzarella cheese and mushrooms. Lady J chose a pasta dish with Bolognese sauce and mushrooms, accompanied by garlic bread. I knew the drive home would be smelly. I chose a ham and mushroom omelette with chips and a side salad. We declared that the meals were fantastic, magnificent and well-made, and to follow, we all had a piece of Black Forest gateau that melted on the tongue. It was beautiful. We had filter coffee and mints after that. Truly a feast.

By now it was almost 6.00 pm and I suggested that we had a drink next door to finish the evening off. Because of her age, Ysabel chose a fresh orange juice which they actually prepared in front of us. Despite having just eaten, she added a bag of crisps to the order leaving me to wonder where she put it all.

Lady J, being the designated (and only) driver, risked a small glass of wine while I, for some strange reason, felt very daring and had a Harvey Wallbanger. As we sat down, I offered two pounds in fifty pence pieces to Ysabel so that she could play on a machine which stood in a corner with lights flashing everywhere and looked like an item of alien technology. With all the whirring sounds that came from it, there was a possibility that I might be right in my guess.

Lady J and I sat at a table and I told her how delighted I was to be home. Suddenly there was an almighty clanging sound and Ysabel ran back to us.

"I've won the jackpot, Daddy, please can you collect it for me?" she said excitedly. I went over and money was still chugging out of the machine to an accompanying cacophony of bells, sirens and trumpet-like sounds. I noticed that the jackpot was fifty pounds so I could understand her excitement. Normally, any machines she played paid out a maximum of five pounds. The noise ceased and I started piling fifty pence pieces into my pockets. "You should have that Daddy. You gave me the money to play", said Ysabel.

"No my sweet, the winnings are yours to do with as you will when we get home again. I'll change it into notes for you. I thank you for the offer though". I told her.

Later at home I gave her fifty pounds from the envelope containing the money that I'd changed back from dollars at the airport from the original twenty thousand I'd been given. A lot remained. Though Bertie had taken back the hundred thousand in bearer bonds, he always left me what remained of the expenses. As he'd supplied the plane tickets there was still about ten thousand left to keep the household going till my next trip, should there be one.

The fifty pence pieces I put in a jar which would be useful at Christmas. Ysabel hugged me and promised to be careful with her spending. I told her just to enjoy it. By about 10:00 pm, the travelling and the day had caught up with me and I said goodnight to the girls. I allowed myself enough time to write this before catching up on my sleep.

Monday, September 5, 1994
The Results

All through this summer we've heard, "It's no good, I know I've failed", from Ysabel. Should that be true she has a promising career as an actress judging by all the drama queen histrionics that have accompanied the statements. Nothing we could say could convince her that she was wrong or that the results didn't matter as long as she'd done her best.

For the last two weeks of August, we'd allowed her to go on holiday with friends to Italy in the hope that it would take her mind off things. The parents of one of her friends have a nice villa over there where the girls couldn't get up to mischief. Of course, the results had arrived while she'd been away. The Great GCSE Debate was about to unfold now that she'd returned and I'm not sure who was more nervous, Ysabel or Lady J and I. Ysabel had tried to convince us both to open the envelope, but we'd both insisted that the honour was hers alone. At last the moment had arrived. She'd got back from the holiday late on the previous day, so we'd propped the envelope up against a teacup on the dining table this morning at breakfast.

We expected a fanfare or a drum roll at least but gritting her teeth, Ysabel tore the envelope open. Julia and I sat there, tense, and watching the expressions on her face for any sign of what was to come, cheers or tears. Unfortunately the last expression, that of open-mouthed shock, was the one that now seemed to be locked on her face as the letter dangled from her hand.

Unable to contain myself further, I extracted the letter from her white knuckled fingers and started to read it.

I didn't seem to be able to speak or react when Lady J removed the letter from my fingers.

"Three A star passes, 3 A passes and 2 B passes", she read out loud. "Not a lot to worry about there is there?" she said.

Ysabel and I came awake together both with rictus grins on our faces.

"Congratulations, darling", I said. "So what's next, maybe the teaching university?"

"No Daddy, I want to take a year out and get a job".

We had been over this many times. Ysabel had oft told us of her desire to teach, but neither I nor Lady J was prepared to push her too much and maybe make her back off from university in rebellion. Still, a year out was a shock.

Ysabel left the table and slowly walked out of the dining room. She must have reached the lounge when suddenly Lady J and I heard a whoop of delight and a scream of "Yeessssss!" echoing down the passageway. It seemed Ysabel's fear of failure had suddenly disappeared. I took out my wallet and started counting notes onto the table.

"What are you doing, David?" asked Julia.

"Paying up as promised, my dear", I replied, "Twenty pounds for each A star, ten pounds for each A and I'll top it up to a hundred for the B passes too. I'd hate to have to pay up when she's confident of her results, if it costs me this much when she thinks she's failed".

"True, my dear", said Lady J. "I'd better start counting too as I made her a similar promise myself. At this rate we'll both be borrowing the housekeeping from her".

Tuesday, September 6, 1994
The Pianist

My eyes opened and I stared into the eyes of my deadliest foe who bristled with weapons. Needless to say it was the cat who'd woken me up and the weapons were his claws, which he was extending and retracting into my neck. I'm sure his eyes were daring me to move and promising me regrets if I did. He was comfortable and that's all that counted.

After what seemed like an hour of our confrontational eyes, he finally got bored and moved himself to a comfortable spot on my stomach, which was well covered by the duvet and protected me from the claws of the demon upon me. I edged up the bed slightly to look at the clock. It read 6:15 am and I silently sent sarcastic thanks to the cat. Edging myself from under him I slid out of bed. Immediately he found the warm spot that I'd vacated and went to sleep. I slipped on my dressing gown and went to make a drink, but to my surprise Lady J was already there drinking a coffee.

"Good morning, my dear", I said. "Bad night?"

"No, dear", she answered, "I just woke up early when the cat used my body as a springboard on his way in to you".

I don't know why but I apologised as though I was responsible for his actions.

"What plans for today, my dear?" I asked.

"Well, I'm going to the stables at 7:00 am to turn the horse out and groom him, then I'll be back in time to take you for your blood test. After that, I think Ysabel wants to go to Barchester to spend her exam money on a new set of clothes".

Inwardly I groaned, as I'd forgotten the blood tests which the doctor had ordered a while ago when he'd found my blood pressure was high. I knew that they'd be checking cholesterol levels, and that my penchant for potatoes and bread in large quantities would not have helped.

At 9:00 am prompt we arrived at the local cottage hospital to have the blood drawn.

"Diet?" asked the nurse.

"What colour?" I replied, trying to lift the mood, and anyway I couldn't help myself.

"Har de har", she said, "as if I hadn't heard that before".

Rebuked, I hung my head and said, "Normal diet, I suppose, with a heavy reliance on potatoes and white bread".

"That stops now", she told me, "no more than two small potatoes from now on and a change to wholemeal bread".

"OK", I sighed, "I'll cut down drastically. Am I allowed treats like chocolate?"

"Not a chance", said she and the sunlight went out of my day.

I went outside to where Lady J and Ysabel were waiting.

"You look like you've lost a pound and found sixpence, Daddy", said Ysabel.

I explained what had been said by the nurse and they sympathised by telling me that I wouldn't be able to join them for chocolate cake with my coffee when we had a break in shopping. I'm sure that I glimpsed slight grins on both faces at that.

We reached Barchester and parked up at a shopping precinct, where there was a large number of the type of shops that Ysabel liked. We got out of the car and followed her as she led us from shop to shop full of unmentionables.

No doubt heaven for her, but hell for me, not knowing where to put my face when asked to give an opinion on prospective purchases.

Lady J and I were given various bags to carry so that we didn't feel useless. When we had about a tree's worth of paper carrier bags we stopped for coffee. It was painful to see them tuck into their cake with such glee, while my stomach grumbled and asked where its share was.

Soon the pace picked up and we were off again. We must have looked at the world's supply of jeans, skirts and tops when Ysabel finally announced she'd finished. With a quiet shout of ‘Hurrah’, I suggested that we look for somewhere to have lunch. Lady J suggested that we go to the Cathedral café which would give us a chance to look around afterwards. We all agreed and headed in that direction.

The café was rather sparse but the small menu did at least have a homemade soup and bread roll on which we settled. Finding a table, we carried the soups over together with our drinks. I had just had my first spoonful of soup when 'plonk', there was someone just settling down at the piano. Thinking nothing of it, I settled down again to my soup when I heard it.... ‘plink, plonk, bum note, plink’. It was awful.

The tunes played were just about recognizable, but interspersed with so many bum notes that I was unable to carry on eating in case I choked with laughter. I glance across at Lady J and that was it – we both struggled to stifle the sound but there was no mistaking the fact that we were laughing. Ysabel joined in, tears in her eyes, and it seemed to be catching table by table like the tide rolling in. Unable to hold it in any longer, one man laughed out loud. The elderly lady on the piano stool looked round but continued playing. As she was unable to see the keys, this did not help improve the cabaret. Her fingers ran over the keys, but did a worse job than before as all her attention was now focused on us. More bum notes came and the laughter got louder and spread more. It seemed to echo from the beams of the ceiling and all the battle flags of local regiments on the walls rippled gently. By now I was really struggling and I certainly wasn't the only one, as the strain of holding the laughter in showed on Lady J's face. There was no chance of me trying more of the soup at that moment.

Just then two of the cathedral's deans entered the room and walked over to our table.

“I'm sorry sir”, said one, “but I'll have to ask you to vacate the cathedral precincts”.

“Pardon?” I asked, a little incredulous.

“We believe that you threaten the dignity of the cathedral, sir”, said number two.

“David”, said Lady J, “I believe it's time we left. Come, dear”.

I followed as we were escorted outside to the sound of the laughter behind us and the continued ‘plink, plonk, bum note, plink’.

Outside, all I could think of to say was, “I never even got to eat my roll”.

“Never mind, Daddy, it was white bread anyway”, said Ysabel, at which we all three burst into laughter, drawing odd looks from passers-by. The only time we had been ejected from somewhere and it had to be a cathedral.

Thursday, July 8, 1999
A Room with a View

The phone trilled early this morning. As I came awake, the cat, who was lying on my chest, stuck his front paws on my lips as though to shush me. I wasn't about to speak, but knowing that two sets of claws could easily be attached to my upper lip, a scream wasn't far away.

Gently my hands moved to lift the paws away so that I could roll out of bed. Too late, I heard Lady J's voice as she answered the phone. As I moved closer to the edge of the bed, I deposited the two paws back on the quilt but not before they had hit out and placed two sets of red lines on my opposing thumbs. Oscar settled down where my body had lain, oblivious to my pain and to the welling of the blood on my thumbs. I ran through, past Lady J, to the kitchen where I knew there were plasters, arms up and thumbs extended like a Roman emperor of old at the Coliseum.

Plasters on, I went to the lounge where Lady J was just putting down the phone. "Bertie will be here at 8:00 am, dear, he says it's urgent".

"Thank you sweetie", I said. "Did he give you any inkling of what he wants?"

"No inkling at all, David, but I suggest you get dressed before he arrives".

Taking the suggestion on board, I returned to my room and got ready while looking jealously at the cat snuggled down in my bed. I had time for a coffee as it was only 7.30 am when I had finished dressing. I made one for Lady J, who came through ready to face the day when I put the kettle on.

“I'll just have this and go and put Pilgrim in his field”, she told me. “You'll no doubt want to speak privately with Bertie”.

“Righto”, was all I replied,

Lady J drank her coffee and left a few minutes before the infamous Rolls Royce appeared, and Bertie got out. He looked quite flustered, a state I'd not seen him in before. He usually appeared quite relaxed and unflustered.

“David”, he said as he came in. “This is urgent and I hope you're free for an immediate departure”.

“I'm free”, I responded, trying very hard not to mimic the very camp catchphrase used in a popular television programme. “As for leaving now, I could do that if I felt the same sense of urgency that you're currently displaying”.

Sitting down, Bertie told me that they (his department) had heard of a threat to Sultan Ibrahim of Beritana, and that he was going to be assassinated. His death would be likely to threaten the oil agreement we had, and the government wanted me to be the one to warn him. Mentioning that I was surprised that no one had just picked up a phone, I said that as I had a fondness for the sultan and his family, I would go right away. Bertie looked relieved for a moment and then regained his usual impenetrable manner.

Lady J arrived home at this point and engaged Bertie in idle chatter while looking directly at me.

“So you're off again today, dear, I'd better pack you a bag”.

I don't know how she knew, as neither of us had said a word.

Bertie stood up to leave and as he did so, he passed me an envelope which contained my plane ticket and a large amount of cash for expenses. He made a small bow to Julia, wished us both goodbye and left.

“Will you be all right on your own, Julia?” I asked, since we had not been apart since Ysabel had left home last year to move into her own flat. “You could come with me if I can arrange it”, I told her.

“Don't be silly, dear”, she responded. “Grizelda could look after Oscar, but who would see to Pilgrim at such short notice? I'll be fine, now let’s get this bag sorted and get you out of my hair”.

Bag sorted and with my passport in hand, Julia ran me to the airport, gave me a quick hug and then departed again for home, leaving me standing where I'd so often stood before, in the departure lounge.

A young man approached and kindly offered to carry my bag to the plane for me. I accepted gratefully.

On the plane, it turned out that we were seated together, and I hoped that that would make the journey all the more pleasant. I was wrong!!

“I say, aren't you Lord David Prosser of the Buthidar Peace Movement?”

“I am indeed”, I responded.

“Well”, he said, “I'm a member but I've been thinking of leaving, as you allow too many foreigners to join”.

“That's the whole point”, I answered. “Peace is something that should be worldwide. Peace is something that should cross all racial barriers”.

“I understand that”, he told me, “but how can you allow our enemies to join and learn about us?”

“We have no enemies”, I told him. “Those who join can see that we have no ulterior motives other than friendship and if they dislike it, and if they don't agree with us, they can leave. Those that stay are committed to the peace between us that I want”.

"I see", he said, "but some of them will not want what we do, they will view our love for peace as a weakness".

"Then they will be disappointed, as our friendship with other people is a strength not a weakness". I closed.

He seemed determined to undermine the arguments and I wondered why someone who feared others so much had joined. But, I hoped that I had argued enough to convince him that we were right and that he could help by bringing others to the cause. I decided not to hold my breath waiting though.

When we departed the plane, I saw him in the airport talking to a group of Hare Krishna followers and trying to convert them as though the Buthidars was a new religion.

I saw Mustapha Phag as I passed through customs and he waved to me. The porter carried my bags to where he stood and I followed.

"Hello, old chap", he said. "Welcome back. I'll put your bags in the car and we'll be off".

"How on earth did you know I was coming?" I asked.

"Sir Bertram phoned the Sultan and asked if he'd mind a visit from you and of course Ibrahim said he'd be delighted. He asked me to pick you up, as a friendly face is always good to see".

"As always, Mustapha, it's a delight to see you", I told him.

We got into the car, and on the journey to Beritana, Mustapha pointed out the same things that he'd pointed out on my previous visit, but each time asking me if I remembered what it was. Luckily I did remember the majority of them, and he seemed pleased.

When we arrived at the palace, Mustapha handed over my bags to a servant and I went to the room that had been readied for my arrival.

“Dinner will be at 6:00 pm, Lord”, said the servant as he departed.

So, at 6 of the clock I was ready and made my way down to the dining room I had known previously. Sultan Ibrahim was there and hugged me. “I'm so glad to see you again, David, and after so long”.

“I'm delighted to be able to return again, Your Highness. I'm grateful for your hospitality. It has been far too long”, I replied.

“You remember Suki, I'm sure”, he said moving aside to reveal a young girl of twelve who had grown to be so pretty, and yet still recognisable as the little child I'd met before.

“Hello, Uncle Daud”, she said, shyly offering her hand to be shaken.

“It's a delight to see you again, Suki”, I said, pulling her into a hug. “I've always remembered my young friend”.

She returned the hug with a chuckle and said “And I remember also the lord who let me sit on his knee and who told me stories”.

We moved around the room to greet people, and Ibrahim explained that his wife Jenny was unwell and wouldn't be joining us. He placed me at his right hand at the low table, at which I felt honoured. Suki took the seat to my right.

I heard a clap of hands and the meal was brought in and placed upon the table. Lamb and rice is a staple dish and I was strangely glad to see that the Sultan shared his people's simple tastes.

During the meal I said nothing to Ibrahim of the reason for my visit. We chatted generally about things of common interest and I was happy that Suki was able to join in. When we discussed art, she showed a good knowledge of painters and styles, and was able to take a leading part in the conversation. I could see from the pride displayed on Ibrahim's face that he adored Suki, and I could see that same love reflected on hers.

As the meal ended, Ibrahim dismissed the servants and leaned back on his cushions. “Suki”, he said, “please go and check on your mother before bed. You shall have a chance to talk to your Uncle Daud tomorrow, but tonight he and I have things to discuss”.

Suki hugged her father and wished him goodnight. She turned to me and told me that she'd be happy to see me in the morning and then she hugged me before turning and leaving the room.

“So, David, it's a delight to have you back here, but I'd be glad to know what situation actually brought you back”.

“Your Highness”, I started, before I was reminded to call him Ibrahim. “I've been informed that there is a plot to assassinate you. It seems not to be the usual palace plotting, and I was sent to warn you of the situation and to help where I can”.

“That is kind, David, and I'm glad it was you they sent, but what help can you be if we don't know where the threat is coming from?”

“If the worst happened, Ibrahim, and an assassin was successful, then I would ensure Jenny and Suki got safely away, knowing that they could not run the country in such circumstances, and also that they may be targets themselves. But, I don't want that to happen. Let’s see first if we can foil this plot. Tell me two things. Firstly, who would inherit your title if you were gone, and secondly, who disagrees the most with the way you run the country?”

“David, I thank you for your concern and for the offer of help. If the worst were to happen, at least I should know that Jenny and my little Suki would be safe. To answer your questions, my cousin Sheikh Rattlnroll would become Sultan on my death as he has a large following. But, we are friends as well as cousins and I think he would run the country in a similar way. His staff seem to be friendly towards me too. As for the second question, that's more complicated. There are two main groups who dislike me. A fundamental group called 'The arms of Allah', who think I am too westernised, and a group of American businessmen who think they could run the oil fields better than the British-trained locals who do it now. They may be right, but it's obviously important to me that my own people do it".

"Thank you Ibrahim. I'd be grateful if I could think on this a little before we speak of it again".

Ibrahim wished me goodnight and we parted, I to my room to complete my journal before sleep, and I now wish you goodnight.

Friday, July 9, 1999
Mustapha Asks a Favor

I awoke fresh this morning and was delighted to find that Ibrahim had arranged for suitable robes to be left for me. They had proved to be comfortable on my last visit. I took a shower and was just washing myself when I heard a voice.

"Good morning, David, I wonder if I may bend your ear for a minute?"

I realised that it was Mustapha and asked if he'd wait until I had finished in the shower. I rinsed myself off and wrapped a towel around me before stepping into the bedroom.

"Good morning Mustapha, what can I do for you, my friend?" I asked.

"David, I don't fully know why you're here, but I've heard that there is a threat to Ibrahim and I want to ask if you're here because of that".

"I came over to warn Ibrahim of a plot, Mustapha, but I stay here as a friend".

"I accept that, David, and I want you to know that I will do anything I can to help you save my Sultan and the kingdom. I shall now go about my duty and ask that we may share any news we hear".

"Gladly", I told him. "Ibrahim is an exceptional man".

Mustapha left, and I dressed and went down to a breakfast of fruit and found Suki waiting for me.

"So, Uncle Daud, I may be too big for your stories now but I hope I will still be able to enjoy your company?"

"Nothing would give me greater pleasure, Suki. Perhaps we could walk together in the Souk today?"

"Wonderful", she said, "I shall be ready when you finish eating".

True to her word, within minutes of breakfast Suki was at my side, and arms linked, we wound our way down to the old town and the souk.

"Tell me of your family, Uncle Daud", asked Suki.

I told her about everyone at home and mimicked some of them for her amusement. She knew that I would want gifts for Lady J and Ysabel and took me to a part of the souk where they made jewellery. I managed to haggle a price on gifts to take home. Accepting the Arab hospitality towards guests, when I had finished my purchase, I risked a stomach ulcer by sharing a cup of the thick, sweet coffee they favour.

Suki was a delight to be with and we spent much of our time in the souk laughing until she asked me point blank why I was here. I was a little taken aback and unable to think of a convincing lie, so I told her the truth - that I'd heard of a threat and was here to help if I could. Suki hugged me and said she wanted to help in any way she could too.

Back at the palace we separated while Suki went for a ride. I was secretly glad to be alone for a few minutes so that I could snoop where I wanted. A little while later, I found Mustapha in the throne room and asked him to tell me about any new staff that had been taken on recently.

"Well", he said, "there has been a new tutor for Suki, a new groom for the Royal stables, a groundsman to look after the small private garden and a new officer in the Royal Guard".

"Thank you, Mustapha. These are people I must look at and we must also ensure that from now on people are checked when they come before Ibrahim for audience".

"I agree", he said, "we must be extra vigilant from now on".

“Yes, but we mustn't arouse suspicions or we'll never catch the assassin”, I told him.

I was left pretty much to my own devices for the rest of the day. Suki had her lessons and obviously Mustapha had his duties. I strolled around the palace, noting places that I thought would be good for an assassin to hide, and generally just saying hello to all the staff to familiarise myself with their faces.

At dinner, Suki sat by me and chatted. She also introduced her tutor who sat at her other side. Ibrahim was opposite me tonight and seemed deep in conversation with Mustapha. There was still no sign of Jenny, and I guessed she was still unwell.

After dinner I excused myself and came up to my room to retire early.

Saturday, July 10, 1999
The Holiday-Day

At breakfast this morning, I was tired as my sleep seemed to have been patchy. This was probably due to the calls from the muezzin to bring the faithful to prayer. Perhaps the sound had carried more this morning, or maybe they knew that I was here and accordingly used a bigger megaphone.

Suki was in the dining room and rose from the table as I entered.

"Uncle Daud", she said. "Today I declare a holiday and I want to spend it with you. After you have eaten, we will go and say hello to Nightshade, yes?"

I agreed gladly and sat down to eat a quick meal of grapes. Picking up two apples, I started to eat one and I put the other in my pocket. Then seeing the impatience on Suki's face, I followed her to the stables to say hello to her beautiful horse.

Nightshade came quickly to the stable door as he heard Suki's voice and snickered at the sight of her. The affection was obvious and mutual as she put her arms around his neck and brought her face up to his. She spoke softly into his ear and then stood back saying, "You can give him the apple you brought for him, Uncle Daud. He knows it's in your pocket and is grateful for your thoughtfulness".

I put the apple in the palm of my hand and offered it. Nightshade nodded his head and neighed as if to say thank you, and then with such care he leaned down and bit the apple in half, chewed, swallowed and picked up the second half. He had been so gentle that I knew I had no need to count my fingers before I left.

Suki and I talked as she groomed Nightshade and refilled his hay net, these being jobs for which I knew staff were paid and which they were willing to do. I knew then that I cared very much for Suki, a princess with no pretensions and who cared for animals and people alike with love. Quite a rare find amongst those who often treated servants with total disdain and contempt. I think my mind must have wandered for a minute until I realised that Suki was tugging on my sleeve.

"Uncle Daud, I am going to trust you with a secret. I know you will tell no one, but as you are so kind to me and my family you should know this". With that, Suki tugged on the hay rack at the back of Nightshade's stall. It tilted as though she'd pulled it off and I moved to catch it. As I did so, there was a clicking sound and part of the back wall slid open.

"Come", she said, "follow me".

I did so and entered a dark passageway, where I promptly tripped over and landed on my hands for support. I heard a small chuckle followed by, "Mind the step, Uncle Daud".

I heard the door slide closed behind me and then with a click there was light.

"We've had electricity installed since this was built, Uncle Daud, though of course we had to kill all the electricians who worked on it", said Suki with a straight face.

My mouth must have opened in shock before she said, "Be careful you don't catch flies like that, my uncle. Actually we just used electricians from abroad to do the job then sent them home, as I hate cleaning up blood". She laughed then and remarked how serious I looked.

"Where does this passageway lead to, Suki?" I asked with a smile at her antics.

"One way is down to the dungeons, one way to the throne room and one to the bedrooms", she answered. "But there are spy holes from the passages to most of the ground floor rooms", she added, which gave me an idea.

"Suki, can you show me all the entrances and exits, please, where all the light switches are, before I fall again, and how to open and close all the doors?"

I could see her wondering if she had made a mistake and if I could be trusted with all this information, but her decision was rapid.

"Of course, Uncle Daud. But... if I do so, you must agree to tell me if you find anything out about who wants to kill my father".

"Deal", I said sticking out a grimy hand from where I'd fallen. Suki ignored the hand and instead came close enough to give me a peck on the cheek and a hug. I hugged her back gladly. This delightfully bright child had made it easy for me to watch people and to see if I could solve the mystery of who wanted the sultan dead.

We spent the rest of the morning going round the ground floor and upper floor passages where Suki showed me all the spy holes and all else that I had asked for. One passageway even opened into my bedroom, and I wondered if Mustapha knew of it and had used it to get into my bedroom previously.

At lunchtime we turned off the lights and exited the passage into the throne room which was empty of people. We then made our way to the dining room, stopping off only long enough for me to wash my hands.

Lunch consisted of cold meats and rice with fruit to follow. Ibrahim was already there with Mustapha and some of his other advisors.

"Ah", he said, "David, I hope my child has not been leading you astray". This was said with an indulgent smile that seemed to be echoed by all in the room.

“No, Your Highness”, I replied. “We've been to see the horses and she's proved to be a mine of information on bloodlines. Nightshade is a beautiful horse”.

“Ah yes, he's the product of the best sire and dam I own”, he told me.

“Much like your own daughter”, I replied.

“Ah, ever the diplomat”, said Ibrahim, “but I thank you for your kind words”. As lunch ended, I beckoned to Mustapha to join me.

“How goes it, old chap?” he asked me.

“Mustapha, I've been thinking about the problem. As I've walked around, I've noticed that the new groundsman is unlikely to come within striking distance of the sultan, and the new groom is also an unlikely suspect unless he specifically manages the Sultan's horse. I've not ruled them out, but think I need to concentrate on Suki's tutor and the new guard. Can you find out for me where they came from?”

“That should be easy, David. I will let you know this evening what information I have”, Mustapha replied.

Suki had lessons that she couldn't avoid during the afternoon, so I walked around the palace, casually asking questions about how other people related to the newcomers. I was especially interested in the opinions of the kitchen staff, as that's where much of the gossip usually goes on.

True to form, I got most of my information there. Opinion said that the groom was nice and was only there because he wanted to marry one of the Sultan's servants. The groundsman was a fool who didn't seem to know his job and who had to be chased by his supervisor to do any work. I found that interesting. The tutor was dismissed as being too nosy because he asked many questions about the palace staff, much as I was doing now, and the guard was seen as strange because he didn't seem to talk much at all.

With the exception of the groundsman, I didn't think that I could rule anyone out at as a potential assassin. I drank coffee with the cooks and told them how much I enjoyed my meals. I listened carefully to all they said and then I saw the new guard enter the kitchen. For all that they said he didn't talk much, he seemed very edgy, and snapped when he spoke to my companions.

"Give me a meal! I am on duty tonight and must eat before I start".

I rose from the table and thanked the staff for their hospitality before I left the room. For the rest of the day before the evening meal, I wandered the palace making mental notes to myself of the best places for an assassin to hide.

At the meal I was able to place myself beside Mustapha, who was able by then to give me a potted history of each of the new staff.

The groom had come from the stables of a local Sheikh to care for a horse that Ibrahim had bought to race. He had cared for the animal since it was born and knew all its funny ways. He wanted to marry one of Jenny's servant girls. That was enough for me to rule him out of my suspicions.

The groundsman was here as a favour to his father, who hoped that being in Ibrahim's service would cure him of his idle ways. His father was a strong supporter of Ibrahim and the changes he tried to make. I thought the father was going to be disappointed if he were to hear the opinions of the kitchen staff, but I at least felt able to also rule the boy out as a suspect, as he was not here of his own volition.

The guard had applied for a job a while ago. He had been taken on when one of the other guards had disappeared from his job. The new guard's parents were wealthy merchants who also supported Ibrahim's reforms.

They had despaired when he had left university in the middle of his course, but were now happy that he was in Ibrahim's employ with a steady job.

The tutor had been a lecturer at the university, but had declared that he now wished for a quieter life. His credentials seemed impeccable.

I thanked Mustapha for his help and moved to speak with Suki. I asked about her lessons that afternoon and what her tutor had talked of.

The meal eventually came to an end and we each went our own way. Before Mustapha left, I asked if he'd be able to meet with me later in my room. I suggested that midnight might be the best time, which caused a raising of his eyebrows before he agreed.

I went to my room to start writing these notes before midnight came.

Sunday, July 11, 1999
Knife in the Night

Early hours.

Mustapha arrived at my door at just past midnight and I thought it was time to let him know my thoughts. I asked him if he would take four of his best men, check on the Sultan's guards, and replace them with two of his own. Following that, I asked him to hold the two replaced guards for a short time until I could question them. I gave him my reasons for the request and he immediately made a phone call to arrange things and left.

I entered the passageway that Suki had shown me, which was connected to my room. After a bit of fumbling, I found the light switch and turning it on, was surprised to find Suki standing there.

"What on earth!" I said. "You nearly gave me a heart attack then. What are you doing out of bed?"

"I saw you talking to Mustapha earlier, and you looked so serious that I feared you had found something wrong. I do not intend to allow harm to come to my father so I waited to see what you were doing this evening".

"OK, Suki. It's possible that I am wrong, but I fear something will happen tonight. You may come but only if you first promise not to get in harm's way", I told her.

Suki agreed and we worked our way along the passages to her father's room. She arrived just ahead of me and put her eye to the peephole.

"Uncle Daud", she screamed. "Quickly!"

I pressed the catch to open the door and ran into the room. Both Jenny and Ibrahim were asleep, but heading towards the bed, wide awake, was a man holding a knife. "Stop!" I cried, jumping at him and I saw his arm move. I felt a pain as I brought him down. The main door opened and in rushed Mustapha and his four men who pounced on us.

As they dragged us apart and Mustapha flipped the lights on, I saw that Ibrahim and Jenny had awoken and were comforting, or being comforted by, Suki. Mustapha said, "You were right, David. This assassin is the guard you suspected. My men found the other guard unconscious outside the room. They will take this man to be interrogated to find out who sent him, but in the meantime I think we need to get you to a doctor".

It was then that I noticed the knife sticking out of my thigh and saw blood pooling on the carpet. All I could think of to say was, "My apologies, Ibrahim, for the mess on your floor. I think solutions are available these days which will eradicate the stain".

Suki came running over. "Oh, Uncle Daud, you're hurt". Then she burst into tears, no doubt of relief at knowing her father was safe.

I found that I could not walk easily and no one wanted to risk moving the knife, so to my embarrassment, I was carried by Mustapha and Ibrahim to my room and a doctor was called.

He came and said it was a hospital I needed, but I felt unable to go and asked him to take out the knife and stitch me up, which he did, admonishing me all the time. He said I was lucky that the artery had not been hit, or it would be the hospital despite any argument from me.

He bandaged me up and also managed to rustle up some old crutches, as he said it was obvious that I wouldn't stay still for long. Suki had stayed with me while the leg was dealt with, but as Ibrahim came back to offer his thanks, after he'd settled Jenny again, I asked him to make sure Suki went and got some rest and suggested that he did the same.

I tried to relax but things kept running around in my head. Eventually I saw things the right way after my fashion and fell asleep.

Later that day

I was woken quite early by a knock at my door. My watch said it was barely 7.00 am as I called out, “Come in”.

It was Mustapha. “Lord David”, he said rather formally, “we owe you a debt of gratitude for saving Ibrahim's life. The guard has confessed that he belongs to a fundamentalist group that disagrees with Ibrahim's aims. He will be dealt with! But tell me, what made you suspect him?”

“The other staff told me that he didn't speak very much, and when I saw him yesterday he was very snappy and seemed on edge, as though he had something on his mind. Last night it was a precaution only to ask for your men, but while he was on duty seemed the most likely time for him to strike if he was indeed our man”.

“Ah”, said Mustapha, “it seems that I should pay more attention to staff gossip. Now David, we must arrange transport home to your family and a suitable reward for saving the Sultan's life”.

“No need for any reward, Mustapha. I count both you and Ibrahim as friends and knowing you're safe is reward enough. Before you do arrange transport though, I have a favour to ask of you”.

“Ask away dear friend”, said Mustapha.

“Can you check for me if the tutor has requested an audience with the Sultan today?” I asked.

“You have me mystified, David, but I will do as you ask before the audiences start. Now, breakfast I think. I'll arrange to have some brought to your room”.

“Most kind, Mustapha”, I said, at which point there was another knock at the door which opened to reveal Suki complete with a breakfast tray.

“I have brought you something to eat, Uncle Daud”, she said, wearing a huge smile. She placed the tray at the end of the bed and came forward to hug me.

“I owe you my father's life, Uncle”, she said, “and I can never repay you”.

“No need, Suki”, I responded, “no need at all”.

Mustapha bowed to me and said, “I can see I'm not needed and breakfast is already brought, so as I have a heavy day, I shall depart if you'll both excuse me”. Saying that he left the room.

Suki sat with me until I had eaten and had drunk my tea. I pushed the tray back to the end of the bed and thanked her. I also asked a great favour which puzzled her, but which she agreed to do for me. Grudgingly passing me my crutches, she led me out of the room and along the corridors to another room. Then, as promised, she waited outside while I entered. I was not long in there and then rejoined her and she helped me downstairs to the throne room carrying my crutches. We found a seat outside, watched by a now observant pair of guards, and I asked Suki to find Mustapha for me.

He returned with her and said he'd been about to come up to my room with the information I wanted and was surprised to find me down there. He confirmed for me that the tutor had an audience and was due to appear in fifteen minutes. Suki looked on in puzzlement while we spoke. Mustapha left to attend his Sultan during the audiences and I asked Suki to bring me two of the Sultan's guards, as I didn't want to take the two from the door.

“What game are you playing, my uncle?” she muttered as she left to fetch the guards.

She soon returned with two that I was pleased to see had been part of last night's contingent. The tutor appeared and nodded to Suki.

"I wish to appraise the Sultan of your progress, my child". he told her. At that moment, Mustapha appeared at the door of the throne room and beckoned the tutor forward. Gathering the two guards and a puzzled Suki I followed him in.

He approached the throne, and with a low bow stopped. As he rose from the bow, I saw that he held a pistol. A hush fell on the room and I held my arms out to prevent my two guards from rushing forward. Two more who flanked Ibrahim rushed forward, although they would have been better standing in front of him, thus allowing him to get up and leave. Ibrahim, with courage, stood and faced the tutor.

"Die, traitor of Islam!" cried the tutor, pulling the pistol's trigger to no effect. I moved forward on my crutches and told the guards to merely restrain him, as I could see that they were itching to kill him.

"Lost something?" I asked, allowing the bullets to trickle through my fingers to the floor. "You are the traitor both to the true meaning of Islam and to your Sultan. I'm afraid when you reach Paradise that the only virgins waiting for you will be Catholic nuns!"

Mustapha, who had tried to throw himself in front of Ibrahim, now came forward with a smile to take the prisoner away. It was the smile of a fox with a key to the hen house, and I hoped that the tutor was very afraid.

Ibrahim came to me. "David, it seems I owe you my life again. This is fast becoming a habit. I do wish you'd warned me in advance though, as I thought my time had come just then. How did you know about him? Come, sit by me".

I manoeuvred myself towards the thrones and sat in Jenny's as Ibrahim sat in his.

“I could not be sure, my friend”, I told him. “The tutor might have had genuine reasons to come before you, but just in case, I searched his room this morning, and when I found a pistol, I removed the bullets. I asked Suki yesterday what lessons this tutor taught and she told me that there had been talk of the eventual dominance of Islam over the infidels. I know enough of Islam to say that it's only the fundamentalists who propound that theory and mean it. I have to admit that I was also suspicious that he had been teaching at the same university which the traitorous guard had attended. It seemed just a possibility that he had actually taught the guard and had plotted this with him”.

“I can never repay what I owe you, friend David, but name whatever you want and it's yours”, Ibrahim told me.

“Your friendship is gift enough, Ibrahim, that and perhaps if you could arrange a comfortable journey home”, I laughed.

Ibrahim stood and I followed. He embraced me and then allowed Suki, who had rushed into the throne room to entwine herself around him, tears in her eyes. After a few moments, during which Ibrahim had held her tightly in return, she turned to me with a twinkle in her eyes and said, “I should pull your crutches away so that you fall, Uncle Daud. You were supposed to tell me when my father was in danger”.

“Alas, dear Suki”, I responded, “I must have let it slip my memory”.

Disentangling herself from her father, Suki hugged me. “My mother would like a word, if you would be so kind”, she told me.

Using the ancient crutches, I limped my way to Jenny's room, where she was sitting up in bed looking a lot better. “David”, she started, “I owe you a huge debt as does the whole country. Ibrahim may be my husband but the majority of his subjects love him too. Thank you. I would like you to take something home for your wife and daughter. Call it a gift from a grateful friend”.

“Your Highness, Jenny”, I said, “I'm glad I was able to do something for you. Julia and Ysabel will be grateful for your gift”.

She passed me two small velvet boxes and told me the smaller of the two was for Ysabel. I placed them in my pocket, bowed and left the room to find Mustapha waiting for me.

“David, my friend”, he said, hugging me. “You have a flight this afternoon. Ibrahim has put his helicopter at your disposal to get you to the airport more quickly and in comfort. You will be met at the other end and conveyed home carefully. I should not want Lady Julia to think that we didn't know how to look after you”.

There was plenty of time to pack and say my farewells to everyone before having to board the helicopter. Ibrahim wasn't able to come to the helipad as he was with Mustapha, making plans to round up the other members of the fundamentalist group. He planned to expel them from his country, although I had said I didn't think that would be enough.

Mustapha had said that he would increase the security around the Sultan and his friends, and I didn't doubt that at all. Suki, however, did come to the helipad and I was surprised when she boarded with me.

“Alas, I have no tutor to give me lessons today since you took him away from me. I have decided to travel to Saudi with you to make sure you leave the country, you troublemaker”, Suki laughed. The flight to the Saudi airport was too quick, and with a last hug Suki and I waved to each other.

I was assisted aboard the plane on the ancient crutches that I had forgotten to return, and settled in the First Class cabin. I slept for most of the journey, and at the other end was placed in a chair and carried off the plane. Passport formalities were mercifully brief and I was wheeled to a waiting Rolls Royce, where a chauffeur stowed my luggage and settled me in the back of the car. We sped homewards and the driver told me that there would be no problems doing so. "I have heard what you did for my Sultan", he told me. "In thanks, I have brought out his official car with diplomatic plates. No one will stop us".

Home at last.

Ysabel was with Lady J and she rushed to the car to help me out. There were cries of "Poor Daddy", and "Can you manage, dear?" as I climbed out and thanked the driver. He wouldn't stay for a cup of tea, informing me he had a hot date waiting at the embassy.

The girls carried my bags indoors and dropped them in the hall, hovering around me until I reached the lounge and flopped on to the couch. Then they placed a cup of tea in my hand and demanded the full story.

That took a fair while as they kept asking questions and then stopping me so that they could make more drinks. I finished the story and asked Ysabel to pass me my small cabin bag. I gave them the gifts from the souk, silver bracelets set with lapis lazuli. They both appeared delighted. Then I passed them the gifts from Jenny, which I hadn't opened. For Julia there was a beautiful ruby necklace which made her gasp. For Ysabel there was a pair of exquisite earrings packed with emeralds. Both gifts were worth a king's ransom, or maybe a sultan's ransom. They were amazed at such generosity.

Soon afterwards I came to bed and promised, after a barrage of nagging, to see Dr. Jekyll the following morning. I had time to complete my diary before sleep.

Monday, July 12, 1999
The Infection

I was woken at 5:00 am when Oscar decided that I owed him some quality stroking time. I saw from his eyes that he was not to be denied and so I stroked, and stroked and stroked. He finally decided that he'd got his due and turning round, he strolled off my chest and along my leg, which brought a gasp from me, and went to settle by my feet. It was now 6:15 am and there was no chance now of falling asleep again, so I got out of bed slowly and carefully before making my way to the bathroom.

I realised that walking was more than uncomfortable, it was really painful and I decided there and then that maybe a visit to the doctor wasn't a bad idea. Accordingly I presented myself at the surgery at 8.30 am when it opened. I blinked and the waiting room was suddenly full. Lady J, who had driven me, went to speak to the receptionist to get me an emergency appointment, while I eased myself into a waiting room chair. I knew that she wouldn't take no for an answer, but was surprised to hear my name called almost straightaway. I limped through to Dr Jekyll's room and saw him smiling. "Right, off with the trousers", he said.

Off they came and I manoeuvred myself onto thc examination table.

"So", he said, "quite neatly stitched, but you have an infection there. I'll give you some antibiotics to clear it. I noticed you were very tentative putting your foot down as you came in. It may be that some tendon damage occurred when the knife entered the muscle. Oh yes, I know all about it, this is a village, remember, where stories travel at the speed of light. I'll get you some proper crutches but it's just possible that you might need them long term".

"Thank you, Doctor", I said, taking the proffered prescription. "I'm afraid I wanted to get home more than I wanted to spend time in a Beritana hospital".

"Understood", he replied, "but that may have been a costly move in terms of healing. Anyway, if the infection doesn't clear, I'll book you in as Long John Silver in this year's village pantomime. Now go to Lady Julia and tell her I said she's to make sure you rest this leg for a few days".

I left the surgery and found Lady J chatting in the waiting room. She excused herself and opened the door for me saying, "It seems as though the whole village knows about your injury and your exploits, dear. I heard one person refer to you as a James Bond character".

Laughing, we made our way to the car and thence to the village chemist to fill my prescription. The staff in there and in the post office, which is inside the chemists, (or is it the chemist which is inside the post office?) are always pleasant and helpful. Liam, who is always efficient, passed over the drugs and said he hoped my leg would soon be better. I swear that there are jungle drums beating, which I can't hear, that keep the whole village aware of any new event.

"Home now, dear", said Lady J. "No more gallivanting for you, I'm afraid. You can help me with village affairs now, like organising the fête".

That last brought a grimace as I'd seen quieter wars than our village fête.

As we arrived home, I saw Bertie's Rolls Royce drawn up by the door.

I found him inside talking to Grizelda over a cup of coffee. She rose to make one for Lady J and me, and Bertie and I withdrew to my office.

“Well, old man. You've really done it this time, haven't you?” he said.

“Pardon, Bertie?” I responded. “I don't quite understand. Done what exactly?”

“Well, you saved Ibrahim's life while you were over there. We thought you'd just boost his security once you'd told him of the threat. And then, after doing it once, you go and do it again publicly. We've had to assure people that you were there as a friend only, and not in an official capacity, in case of reprisals here from the radical element. Now Ibrahim wants to award you a medal in 'The Most Noble Order of the Eagle of Beritana'. No westerner has ever been awarded one”.

“I only did what I could, Bertie, and my actions were more of an accident than anything”, I said.

“Nonsense”, retorted Bertie. “I heard from both Ibrahim and Mustapha on the subject and they were both perfectly clear about your actions. I'm only sorry that as our unofficial envoy we can't give you any recognition”.

“I'm frankly quite relieved”, I told him. “I'm just happy that Ibrahim is safe. It was quite a worrying time for his family”.

“Well, David, needless to say we're all grateful for what you've done and wish you a speedy recovery with the leg. I'll let you know when Ibrahim wants to present the medal”.

“I'd much rather you thanked him for the honour he does me, but would suggest that he wait until I return again to Beritana and do it there, very quietly”.

“I'll suggest that, old chap. Now I must depart and get back to the office. You will take care won't you?” he asked.

I saw Bertie to the door and waved as he left. I took the remains of my coffee to the lounge to find Lady J. She rushed to get a footstool for my leg as I sat down.

"Enough excitement for one day, dear. You relax with a book or the crossword while I see about lunch with Grizelda. She wants to do something special for our wounded hero".

All I could do was chuckle and say, "I suppose I don't have a leg to stand on here, do I?"

The Author, Lord David Prosser, lives in a small village in Wales. He is surrounded by the characters from this book and of course has attempted to disguise their real names in order to protect the innocent or, in reality, to avoid being sued. The cat, however has already taken action against him for using his real identity in the first book in this series (*My Barsetshire Diary*, available on Amazon.com). His wife and daughter maintain a stranglehold on his credit cards for what they call his abuse of, and liberties taken with their fine characters. Please, reader, recommend this book to friends and buy it as gifts for Christmas and birthdays so that His Lordship may remain solvent.

www.ingramcontent.com/pod-product-compliance
Ingram Content Group UK Ltd.
Pitfield, Milton Keynes, MK11 3LW, UK
UKHW040602210726
13854UKWH00008B/1810

9 781447 511816